FEDERAL HILL
FLAVORS AND KNOWLEDGE

Walter Potenza

*History, Traditions and Recipes of
One of the Oldest Italian Colonies
in North America*

POTENZA PRESS

FEDERAL HILL
FLAVORS AND KNOWLEDGE

POTENZA PRESS
286 Atwells Avenue
Providence, Rhode Island 02903
phone: 401-273-2652
fax: 401-273-6879
website: www.chefwalter.com
e-mail: feedback@chefwalter.com

Cover and page design by Kimberleá Weeks.
Printed by Sexton Printing, Inc., St. Paul, Minnesota.

ISBN 0-9700149-0-2

Printed and bound in the United States of America.

Alessandro, Walter and Mamma Elda leaving Italy on July 1, 1972.

DEDICATION

**Dedicated to the ones
who crossed the ocean
with a suitcase filled
with dreams........as I did.**

ACKNOWLEDGEMENT

I will be forever grateful to Signor Joseph R. Muratore for his support and contribution in the making of this book. His knowledge and wisdom made the task much simpler and more exciting. Mister Muratore is a first generation Italo-American. A banker turned historian, he has written and published two books on the Italian Americans in Rhode Island. He has been a contributing columnist to several Italo-American newspapers and among one of his series has been "Landmarks of Federal Hill". He has been a board member of the Roger Williams College, the Community College of Rhode Island and Rhode Island College. He has been the Italian Vice-Consul for Rhode Island. Decorated three times by the Republic of Italy, he has recently received the highest title that country bestows on civilians: Grande Ufficiale. He has also received dual decoration by the Dominican Republic for his study and research on Christopher Columbus. The photographs and bylines in this book are from his private collection.

A special thanks to my wonderful staff who have tested hundreds of recipes: Jill Conklin, New York; Jamon Harper, Barbados; Erin Armour, Rhode Island and Carmela Natale for all the coordinating!

My deepest gratitude to my two daughters, Bianca and Alessandra, for their loving support.

Il PAESE

The turn of the century became a time of transition for food and traditions. Specialties such as lentils, polenta, calamari and baccalá were peasant foods with which Italians were familiar and were accustomed to eating, but were also foods which estranged them from other nationalities. These foods were not available in local grocery stores or listed on restaurant menus. As Italian communities gathered together and developed in sections of cities, food was only one, yet a primary factor in bringing immigrants together. Also important in developing the bond of the heritage were the church, the language barrier, and the comfort of knowing neighbors who could speak the same language.

The very name 'Federal Hill' developed through the years, and although unclear historically, some believe that it was so called because the Federal troops camped on what is today the area around the State House. Others have different versions, yet it is certain that Federal Hill started on Spruce Street. Spruce Street runs parallel to today's Federal Hill, Atwell's Avenue, but at the beginning of the century it was the cradle of the Rhode Island Italian Colony or 'Little Italy' as it is commonly called.

Very few streets are entitled to such recognition: to Rhode Islanders it is the equivalent to what Mulberry Street means to New York, or the North End to Boston. It was on this very street one hundred years ago that many noted men and women began their way in the New World and created a future for their families based on solid ethical traditions.

The first group of Italian immigrants settled on Federal Hill in 1870 and continued until 1910. In the early days of settlement, not only in Rhode Island but throughout the United States, the church was the focal point. Due to the severe handicap and to obstacles created by the lack of knowledge of the English language, most immigrants relied on the pastor for the translation of letters, documents, birth certificates and referral of doctors and undertakers, and for the most important factor, that of job placement. The pastor quickly became the most prominent member of this new community, and the one who held together a new society built around customs and traditions.

The first church on Federal Hill was organized in 1889 on Knight Street with the name Holy Ghost. Reverend Luigi Paroli was the first pastor in 1901, and the corner stone was laid and dedicated by Bishop Scalabrini who came from Piacenza for the dedication. Reverend Flaminio Parenti was the second Pastor in 1922, and during his term the church filled the needs of over 100,000 immigrants. Father Parenti served as pastor for 40 years until 1964 at which time he was named Pastor Emeritus and succeeded by reverend Joseph Invernizzi. Aside from Holy Ghost Church on Federal Hill, another event made a great contribution to the immigrants: the forming of the Scalabrini order, which realized the need for another Catholic Church. The Holy Ghost parish was divided and the Church of Mt. Carmel was then founded in 1921, with one of the most prominent leaders being Monsignor Galliano J. Cavallaro. Mostly Tuscans, Marzanesi, Frosolonesi and other immigrants from the island of Ischia lived near the Mt. Carmel Church at the end of Spruce Street. At the end of the street near the Rectory, the first soda company in Rhode Island was created, along with a bank owned by Nicola Caldarone in 1897.

Spruce Street inevitably became the center for all activities from doctors' offices to bars where Italians would spend their time reminiscing about their motherland and dreaming of a comfortable future. Many politicians and lawyers met daily to discuss all the worldly problems, and many of them made a solid contribution to Rhode Island in their respective fields: immigrants such as Signor Pesaturo who ran an office specifically to guide the great number of immigrants pouring into Providence every week. On the other end, Mrs. Pesaturo taught Italian, the first woman in Rhode Island to teach the language.

While reflecting upon this history, it's amazing how many Italians worked so hard to make the lives of other immigrants much easier and to open the doors to the New World. Today, Federal Hill is a national attraction where people meet to enjoy great food; a place where film directors prepare the next Oscar-winner; a place where nothing has changed: the small stores, the family gatherings, and the churches. Most importantly, Federal Hill delivers the sense of safety and of community that our noble ancestors felt in 1870. May this heritage forever live!

Joseph R. Muratore
Commendatore
Grande Ufficiale della Republica Italiana

BACCALA' ALLA ROMAGNOLA

Salted Cod in the Style of Romagna

Yield: 4 servings

Ingredients

2 pounds	dried codfish (available at specialty stores)
	flour for dredging
4 tablespoons	unsalted butter
2 tablespoons	extra virgin olive oil
1 clove	garlic, minced
3 tablespoons	fresh parsley, minced
	salt and pepper to taste
1 large	lemon, juiced

Preparation

Place the cod in a deep dish, add cold water to cover, and let fish soak for two days in the refrigerator to allow fish to "plump up". Change the water several times.

Rinse and dry the fish and cut it into 2" chunks.

Dredge the fish in flour, shaking off the excess. In a large skillet, heat 2 tablespoons of the unsalted butter and the olive oil. Add fish pieces and brown well on all sides over medium-high heat. Sprinkle fish with minced garlic and parsley and stir the mixture gently.

Cut the remaining 2 tablespoons unsalted butter into bits and add it to the pan. Sprinkle fish with salt and pepper.

Squeeze lemon juice over fish.

BACCALA ALLA ROMAGNOLA

From the Dutch word kabeljauw, which became bacalhau among Portuguese sailors of the 16th century who developed the technique. Later adapted by the Italians, and today one of the staples of Italian traditional cuisine.

PASTA CARBONARA

Bacon and Egg with Pasta

Yield: 4 servings

Ingredients

8 ounces	sliced bacon (about 10 slices) cut into 1" pieces
8 ounces	dry thin pasta, such as capellini or vermicelli
2 cups	heavy cream
1/4 cup	fresh chives, minced
4	egg yolks
1 cup	Pecorino cheese, grated

PASTA CARBONARA

The use of bacon in the place of Pancetta (cured pork belly) is common among Italo-Americans. Authentic Carbonara is made with Pancetta, which is much sweeter and has no cream. This dish was invented by a radical group of the 19th century "I Carbonai " or coal miners located in the western area of Abruzzo.

Preparation

In a large fry pan, cook bacon over medium heat until crisp, adding chives towards end of cooking. Spoon off and discard all but 3 tablespoons of the drippings; keep bacon warm over low heat.

In a 6 quart pan with three quarts boiling water cook pasta al dente, or until just tender to the bite: 3 minutes for dry capellini, 8-10 minutes for dry vermicelli, or cook according to package directions. After adding the pasta to the boiling water, spoon 1/2 cup of the cream into each of 4 wide, shallow bowls. Place bowls in a 200° F. oven while completing cooking.

Drain pasta well, and add to chives and bacon in the pan. Mix lightly, using two forks.

Spoon an equal portion of pasta mixture into each of the warm bowls. Make a nest in the center of each; slip in an egg yolk. Mix each portion individually and sprinkle with cheese. Serve immediately.

MERLUZZO AL LIMONE

Baked Whiting with Lemon

Yield: 6 servings

Ingredients

3 pounds	Whiting or Hake, cut into 6 serving pieces, 3/4" thick
	salt and black pepper to taste
1 teaspoon	paprika
2 cloves	garlic, minced
1/4 cup	fresh Italian parsley, minced
1/2 cup	seasoned breadcrumbs
2 small	lemons, sliced
1 tablespoon	unsalted butter

Preparation

Preheat oven to 375° F. Sprinkle both sides of fish with kosher salt and pepper and paprika. Place fish in a buttered shallow baking dish and sprinkle with garlic, parsley and breadcrumbs. Place lemon slices on fish and add water almost to cover fish.

Bake uncovered 20-30 minutes until fish is firm and crumbs are golden brown. Remove lemon slices, dot with unsalted butter and place under broiler until browned.

They said: By the end of 1905, almost 20,000 Italians were living on Federal Hill, one-tenth of the population of the city of Providence. Most had come in the 1900 and lived in tenements so close to each other that chain link fences were needed to divide properties.

MERLUZZO AL LIMONE

Atlantic cod was usually salted and dried as baccala'. The Mediterranean species is called Nasello. On Federal Hill they used Hake, purchased from the Capitone fish store.

GNOCCHI DI PATATE

Basic Potato Gnocchi

Yield: 8 servings

Ingredients

8 medium	whole potatoes, skin-on, washed
1 large	egg yolk
1 tablespoon	salt
2-2 1/2 cups	all-purpose flour
1 tablespoon	vegetable oil
1/4 cup	unsalted butter
1/2 cup	Parmigiano Reggiano cheese, grated

Preparation

Puncture potatoes in several places with a fork. Bake 1 hour in a 350° F. oven or until tender. Remove and discard skins while warm. Mash potatoes with a fork in a large bowl, and let cool a little. Add egg yolk, salt, and 2 cups flour. Mix well. Knead dough on work surface or board into a ball. It should be soft and a little sticky. If it's too sticky, add a little flour. Lightly flour surface and hands. Break dough into egg-size pieces. Roll to thickness of thumb. Cut roll into 1" pieces. Push each gnocchi against the back of a fork to pattern. This helps gnocchi to absorb more sauce (and makes them a little prettier).

GNOCCHI DI PATATE

Usually made with potatoes in Southern Italy and with ricotta cheese in the North, the word 'gnocco' is also used for someone afflicted by laziness.

Arrange them on a floured tray. Fill a large saucepan 2/3 with salted water. Bring to a boil. Add oil and gnocchi. Stir gently to prevent sticking to bottom of pan. When they float to the surface, let them cook 10-12 seconds more. Remove with a slotted spoon as soon as they are done, as they get soggy if overcooked. (Gnocchi absorb more moisture than regular pasta).

Serve with unsalted butter and Parmigiano Reggiano cheese with leaves of fresh sage, or with your favorite sauce.

FAGIOLI E SALSICCE ALLA LUCANA

Beans and Sausages

Yield: 6 servings

Ingredients

1 tablespoon	extra virgin olive oil
3	sausages, hot Italian
3	sausages, sweet Italian
4 cloves	garlic, minced
1 tablespoon	fresh sage, or 1 teaspoon dried
1 can (28 oz.)	Italian plum tomatoes, drained and chopped
2 cans (36 oz.)	Cannellini beans, rinsed and drained
	salt and pepper to taste

Preparation

Heat oil in an oven proof, flameproof medium casserole and sauté sausages 15 minutes. Drain off excess fat. Add garlic and fresh sage and sauté until garlic is golden. Cool sausages and slice into 1 1/2" pieces. Add tomatoes and beans to casserole and simmer until well cooked, about 15 minutes, stirring occasionally. Season to taste.

Note: This may be held in oven for 30 minutes at 300° F.

FAGIOLI E SALSICCE ALLA LUCANA

This dish is originally from the region of Basilicata, birthplace of the famous sausage Luganega. The people of Basilicata are better known as Lucani. Many of my countrymen came from Basilicata. Their cucina very rarely showcased seafood, due to the fact that it borders with Puglia, Calabria and Campania. However, their contribution to the art of sausages and salami making has been outstanding. Even the old Emperors of Rome wrote about the sausages of Lucania, which we find today in many other regions.

FEGATIELLI IN MARSALA

Chicken Liver in Wine

Yield: 4 servings

Ingredients

1 pound	chicken livers, fresh
1/4 cup	unsalted butter
1/2 teaspoon	salt
1/4 teaspoon	black pepper
1/2 teaspoon	fresh sage
2	slices Prosciutto, diced
8	bread triangles, sautéed
1/4 cup	Marsala wine
1 tablespoon	unsalted butter

Preparation

Cut livers in half, and simmer in melted butter with seasonings and Prosciutto for 5 minutes. Remove livers; place on sautéed bread triangles

Add wine to pan gravy; cook 3 minutes. Add remaining butter, mix well, and pour over livers.

They said: Most immigrants arriving in the beginning of the century had two strikes against them: they were Catholic and they did not speak any English.

FEGATIELLI IN MARSALA

Fresh chicken livers could be purchased from the local chicken vendor on what is today De Pasquale Plaza. Upon entering the store you could see the huge buckets of freshly selected liver resting on an ice block, previously chiseled.

BRUSCHETTA PICCANTE

Spicy Bruschetta

Yield: 4 servings

Ingredients

3/4 teaspoon	red wine vinegar
1/4 cup	extra virgin olive oil
6 tablespoons	fresh parsley, chopped
3 tablespoons	fresh basil, chopped
1/2 teaspoon	garlic, minced
1/8 teaspoon	red pepper flakes
2 tablespoons	fresh breadcrumbs, if needed
6 slices	Italian country-style bread, cut 3/4" to 1" thick, halved
1 tablespoon	extra virgin olive oil

Preparation

Whisk together vinegar and oil. Stir in parsley and fresh basil. Add garlic and pepper flakes. Leave for 2 hours to allow flavors to blend. If the mixture seems too thin, add breadcrumbs. Grill or toast the bread slices. While still warm, brush slices with a little extra virgin olive oil, spread with the bruschetta topping & serve.

BRUSCHETTA PICCANTE

Bruschetta has always been a way to salvage stale bread by simply adding oil and seasonings.
Sometimes the bread is completely immersed in oil, and occasionally it is mixed with a blend of water and vinegar.
The word derives from the Abruzzese "brusca", which means lightly burnt. I make my Bruschette with any kind of bread, but I prefer thick country bread because of the limited amount of yeast incorporated in the dough.

PANZEROTTO

Calzone

Yield: 4 servings

Ingredients

1 cup	warm water
1/2 teaspoon	sugar, granulated
1 package	active dry yeast
3 cups	all-purpose flour, sifted, divided in half
2 tablespoons	extra virgin olive oil
1/2 teaspoon	salt, kosher
12 ounce	mozzarella cheese, shredded or diced
6 ounces	creamy goat cheese
3 ounces	sliced Prosciutto or cooked ham, cut into strips
3 tablespoons	chopped chives
1 tablespoon	fresh garlic, minced
2 tablespoons	Parmigiano Reggiano cheese, grated

Preparation

Combine water and sugar in large bowl; sprinkle with yeast. Let stand 5 minutes to soften.

PANZEROTTO

This name derives from the word "Pancia", or lower stomach, due to the rounded shape at the top. The typical panzerotto is originally from the Lazio region. Italo-Americans eventually created many different fillings for the dough. I've just recently enjoyed one filled with crab meat-unquestionably New England.

Add 1 1/2 cups flour; beat with electric mixer until smooth. Stir in oil and kosher salt. Gradually blend in enough of remaining flour with wooden spoon to make a moderately stiff dough.

Turn out onto lightly floured surface; knead until smooth. Return to bowl; cover and let rise in warm place until doubled. Punch down dough; divide into 3 equal portions.

Roll one portion on lightly floured surface to 9-inch circle. Place 1/3 of mozzarella on one side of dough; dot with 1/3 of goat cheese and top with 1/3 of Prosciutto.

Repeat with remaining dough, cheeses and Prosciutto. Mix chives and garlic; sprinkle over filling.

Moisten edges of dough with water and fold over to enclose filling, pressing edges firmly together. Place on lightly greased baking sheets. Let rise 30 to 45 minutes or until dough feels light to the touch.

Cut slit in each calzone to allow steam to escape. Preheat oven to 375° F. Bake 30 to 35 minutes or until browned. Remove from oven; brush tops with oil. Sprinkle each with 2 teaspoons grated Parmigiano Reggiano cheese.

Serve warm.

They said:
In an article published in 1907
the Providence Journal stated that Providence
had the best Italian colony in the United States,
thanks to an unusually high percentage of doctors,
professors and other members of the better class.

SCALOPPINE AI FUNGHI

Chicken Cutlets with Mushrooms

Yield: 6 servings

Ingredients

1 pound	chicken breasts, boned and skinned
2 tablespoons	flour, salt and fresh ground pepper
1 large	egg, with two tablespoon water
1 1/2 cups	fresh breadcrumbs
4 tablespoons	extra virgin olive oil
2 tablespoons	unsalted butter

SCALOPPINE AI FUNGHI

Scaloppina is a thin pounded piece of meat, generally sautéed very quickly and blended with a variety of vegetables. In this case we call it cutlet, although the true cotoletta has a bone attached to the meat.

Preparation

Pound chicken between sheets of waxed paper until thin.

Combine flour, salt and pepper in pie plate. Beat egg with water in shallow dish. Dredge meat in flour mix, dip in egg mixture, and then roll well in breadcrumbs. Rest the chicken for 15 minutes, to avoid for breading to adhere.

Heat oil and unsalted butter in large skillet over medium high heat.

Add meat in batches and sauté until browned, turning once, about 3 to 5 minutes. Add more oil and unsalted butter if necessary. Keep warm and spoon mushroom sauce over to serve.

They said: Federal Hill had many stores and meat markets. The most versatile was "Joe's Quality", right in the middle of the Hill. The owner Signor Giuseppe DiGiglio was a pleasant and giving man. I remember helping him shovel his driveway one winter, and the next day he came over with the most amazing steaks I had ever seen. It was the blizzard of 78, and I think I must have eaten steaks for 10 days.

CAPONATA DI MELANZANE

Vegetable Spread

Yield: 6 servings

Ingredients

6 tablespoons	extra virgin olive oil
2-1 1/4 pound	each eggplant, cubed
	water with coarse salt
1 clove	garlic, minced
4 large	sweet red peppers, julienned
1 large	onion, thinly sliced
1	hot red pepper pod
2 cups	fresh tomatoes, peeled, seeded and chopped
2 teaspoons	oregano, dried
2 tablespoons	capers, drained
3	anchovy fillets, chopped
1/4 cup	olives, green and black, finely chopped

Preparation

Cut the eggplant into cubes; do not peel. Place the cubes in a bowl covered with abundant water with some coarse salt. Set aside for about 30 minutes. Meanwhile, peel and coarsely chop the tomatoes.

Heat a large saucepan over medium heat. Add the oil and heat. Add onion and garlic and sauté until translucent. Add peppers and cook until wilted. Add eggplant cubes and cook for 15 minutes.

Add the tomatoes, season with salt, pepper and oregano, and cook until peppers and eggplant are tender but not mushy.

Add the capers, olives and anchovies. Remove from heat and let stand at room temperature for several hours.

CAPONATA DI MELANZANEA

Caponata is a Sicilian vegetable dish; in Piedmont a similar dish is called caponet. The word may derive from the Latin " Caupo", tavern, suggesting the kind of robust combinations served in taverns or trattorie.

POLLO TONNATO

Chicken Tonnato

Yield: 6 servings

Ingredients

4 1/4 cups	fresh chicken stock
6	chicken breast halves, skinned
1/2 cup	mayonnaise
1/4 cup	dry white wine
4 flat	anchovy fillets
1 tablespoon	oil from anchovies
1 can (7 oz.)	water packed tuna, drained
2 tablespoons	fresh lemon juice
1/4 teaspoon	oregano, dried
	salt and black pepper to taste
1 tablespoon	capers, drained for garnish
2 tablespoons	fresh parsley, chopped for garnish
1 small	lemon, sliced for garnish

POLLO TONNATO

A variation of the famous Vitello Tonnato made with veal, perhaps of Borghese traditions, it was always served at gala dinners in the Quirinale Palace in Rome.

Preparation

Bring 4 cups chicken stock to boil in covered saucepan. Poach chicken breasts 15 minutes and allow to cool in stock.

For tonnato sauce: In blender or processor, combine mayonnaise, wine, 1/2 cup stock, anchovies, oil from anchovies, tuna, lemon juice and oregano and process until well blended.

Season to taste with kosher salt and pepper.

Remove bones from chicken breasts and cut meat into 1/2" thick slices. Layer on serving platter, overlapping slightly. Pour tonnato sauce over chicken slices and sprinkle with capers and parsley and garnish with lemon slices.

Serve cold, or at room temperature during summer months.

POLLASTRELLO ALLA CACCIATORA

Chicken Hunter's Style

Yield: 6 servings

Ingredients

1/4 cup	extra virgin olive oil
6 pieces	fresh whole chicken (legs with thighs attached and breast halves)
1 1/4 cups	all-purpose flour, seasoned with 1 teaspoon of paprika, salt and black pepper to taste)
1/2 cup	onion, thinly sliced
2 medium cloves	garlic, minced
2/3 cup	Marsala wine
1	green bell pepper, julienne
2	carrots, thinly sliced
1 stalk	celery, thinly sliced
1 cup	canned crushed Italian plum tomatoes
1 teaspoon	dried fresh basil
1 teaspoon	dried thyme
1 teaspoon	dried oregano
	salt and black pepper to taste

POLLASTRELLO ALLA CACCIATORA

Although the term Cacciatora refers to a dish made simply with tomato and fresh herbs, here we offer a variation: a testimony of the casual and pleasant bastardization of the original Italian Cucina blended with the new land.

Preparation

Heat oil in heavy large skillet. Coat chicken with seasoned flour, shaking off excess. Brown chicken on all sides over moderate heat, being careful not to crowd skillet. Remove and set aside.

In the same skillet, sauté onion and garlic for 3 minutes. Turn heat to high and add wine, scraping up browned bits from bottom of skillet. Add chicken, vegetables and herbs. Cook 5 to 7 minutes.

Cover and simmer until tender, about 30 minutes. Add herbs. Adjust seasoning to taste.

PULLASTRO SCARPARIELLO

Chicken of the Shoemaker

Yield: 6 servings

Ingredients

1 small	bunch arugula, fresh
1/4 cup	extra virgin olive oil or salad oil
1 large	red bell pepper, julienne
2 medium	garlic cloves, crushed
2 1/2 pounds	chicken, cut in serving pieces
1 pound	Italian sausage links (sweet or hot), cut crosswise in half
3/4 pound	fresh, white mushrooms, sliced
1 medium	onion, sliced
1/4 teaspoon	dried rosemary leaves, finely chopped
1 cup	chicken broth (fresh or canned)
1/2 cup	dry white wine
1 package (8ounce)	linguine pasta
2 tablespoons	all-purpose flour

PULLASTRO SCARPARIELLO

Probably of Southern Italian origins, I believe this dish is better known in Italian-American kitchens than in Italy.

Preparation

Rinse arugula well; pat dry. Reserve half of the arugula for garnish; discard tough stems from remainder. Thinly slice the prepared arugula and set aside. In a large skillet, heat 2 tablespoons oil over medium-high heat. Add red pepper; sauté until tender. Add sliced arugula and half the garlic; sauté until arugula is wilted. Transfer vegetables and pan drippings to a bowl. In the same skillet, heat remaining oil. Add chicken and sausage in batches; brown on all sides, removing pieces to a plate as they brown.

Discard all but 2 tablespoons drippings from pan. To hot drippings in pan add mushrooms, onion and remaining garlic; sauté until tender. Return chicken and sausage to skillet.

Add 1/2 teaspoon kosher salt, the rosemary, 1/8 teaspoon pepper, the broth and wine. Bring to a boil; lower heat and simmer, covered, until chicken is tender, about 25 minutes.

Meanwhile, prepare linguine according to package directions. Drain; return to pan. Add red pepper mixture; heat through. Toss to combine. Cover and keep warm. Remove chicken and sausage from skillet; arrange on warm serving platter. Skim fat from mixture in skillet. In a small glass measure, mix flour with 1/4 cup water until blended. Stir into liquid in skillet. Bring to boil, stirring constantly. Boil for 1 minute, stirring, until mixture thickens. Spoon sauce over chicken and sausage. Arrange pasta on platter with chicken. Garnish with remaining arugula.

The fruit man, when peppers were 10 cents a dozen, this was a typical vendor who lined Balbo Avenue, today De Pasquale Avenue, along the Cappelli Buildings, where the stands became permanent stands. Excellent fruit and vegetables could be purchased at the most reasonable prices anywhere, as there was no rent, no electricity, no employees to pay. It was a livelihood for those vendors who sold at these stands. This photo was taken in 1932. In 1972, the son of the vendor, realizing the hardships these vendors had endured, had a plaque erected at the very location. That this vendor sold his wares at. The plaque was inscribed as follows:

"On the location stood the fruit stand of my father, with qualities of gold. 1930 to 1962"

POLLO ALLO STILE DI CHIOGGIA

Chicken Chioggia Style

Yield: 4 servings

Ingredients

1 pound	ripe tomatoes
1	chicken (3 to 3 1/2 pound)
	flour for dredging
4 tablespoons	extra virgin olive oil
1 small	onion, halved and sliced
1 stalk	celery, sliced
1/2 cup	dry white wine
1/2 teaspoon	chopped fresh oregano or 1/4 teaspoon dried
	salt and black pepper to taste
2 tablespoons	balsamic vinegar
1/4 pound	fresh domestic mushrooms, sliced

POLLO ALLO STILE DI CHIOGGIA

Chioggia is a town known for its fresh seafood and lovely beaches, a favorite get-away for the Italians during Ferragosto.

Preparation

Remove core from tomatoes and cut a cross in the opposite end. Put into boiling water for a few seconds to loosen skins. Peel, cut in half crosswise and squeeze out seeds. Chop and set aside. Wash and dry chicken; cut into serving pieces, discarding neck, back and wing tips; dredge lightly in flour. Heat olive oil in a large sauté pan, and brown chicken lightly on both sides. Add onion and celery and cook for 2 minutes.

Add the wine, oregano and tomatoes; season with kosher salt and pepper. Cover, and let simmer gently for 30 minutes, turning chicken once. Add the Balsamic vinegar and mushrooms; cook for another 5 to 10 minutes. Check seasoning and serve with Arborio Risotto.

BRODO DI PASSATELLI

Chicken Soup & Passatelli

Yield: 8 cups

Ingredients

8 cups	homemade chicken broth
2 large	carrots, chopped
1 stalk	celery, chopped
2 cloves	garlic, peeled and crushed
1 teaspoon	salt
1 1/2 cups	fresh breadcrumbs, plain
2/3 cup	Parmigiano Reggiano cheese, grated
1 teaspoon	freshly grated nutmeg
2 large	eggs, whole
1 cup	chopped fresh parsley

BRODO DI PASSATELLI

The word derives from "passato", or passed through. The Marchigiani folks add spinach and ground veal to the mixture. In the city of Pesaro ground beef is added. Passatello also refers to elder because the soup is easy digestible and served in old age homes.

Preparation

Pour chicken broth into a large pot and bring to a boil. Add carrots, celery, garlic and kosher salt. Reduce the heat to medium-low and simmer for 30 minutes. Meanwhile, in a mixing bowl combine breadcrumbs, cheese and nutmeg.

Make a well in the center and add eggs; mix until thoroughly combined. The dough should be damp but firm. If necessary, incorporate additional breadcrumbs or a few drops of water; if the dough is too wet or too dry it will crumble. To form the passatelli, pinch off a piece of dough and roll it to approximately 1/4" thickness, then break it into 1/2" lengths. Continue forming the rest of the dough in the same manner. Bring the broth back to a boil, add the passatelli and parsley and cook for 5 minutes. Ladle the soup into bowls, sprinkle with Parmigiano Reggiano and serve.

CIUPPIN LIVORNESE

Seafood Stew

Yield: 8 servings

Ingredients

24	clams or mussels
1 tablespoon	cornstarch
3 small	lobsters, or 3 Dungeness crabs, cracked
1/2 cup	extra virgin olive oil
2 cloves	garlic, minced
2 small	onions, chopped
6	scallions, chopped
3 stalks	celery, chopped
1 large	green bell pepper, chopped
1 teaspoon	fresh thyme, chopped
1	bay leaf
2 cups	fresh tomatoes, chopped
1 can (16 oz.)	plum tomatoes
2 cups	white wine, dry
1 teaspoon	crushed fennel seed
	generous pinch saffron
1/4 cup	fresh parsley, minced
	salt and black pepper to taste
32 small	shrimp, shelled, cleaned
2 pounds	red snapper; fresh, cut into pieces
1 clove	garlic, mashed
1 teaspoon	anchovy paste (optional)

Preparation

Soak clams and mussels in a large pot of cold water with cornstarch.

Drain several times in cold water. Clean and cut lobsters or crabs into pieces. Crack as needed. Heat olive oil in a large pot and add cloves, garlic, onions, celery, bell pepper, thyme, bay leaf, tomatoes, wine, fennel seed, saffron, parsley and kosher salt and pepper. Cook 5 minutes. Add shrimp and snapper, and cook, covered, stirring once, for 5 minutes. Mash 1 clove garlic with anchovy paste and stir into stew. Cook 5 more minutes or until the snapper is soft and the shellfish is open. Drizzle olive oil over the top.

Serve with garlic bread.

CIUFFETTI AI PORCINI

Pasta with Porcini Mushrooms

Yield: 4 servings

Ingredients

1 pound	Ciuffetti or similar tightly - spiraled pasta
6 ounces	fresh porcini mushrooms or (2 ounces dried)
1 cup	heavy cream
4 ounces	unsalted butter
3/4 cup	dry white wine
2	cloves garlic
8 large leaves	fresh basil, chopped
1/4 cup	Parmigiano Reggiano cheese, grated
	pinch marjoram
	salt and black pepper to taste

Preparation

Sauté garlic in unsalted butter till it becomes translucent. Add porcini mushrooms, thinly sliced, wine and marjoram, kosher salt and pepper to taste. When wine and water completely evaporate, add cream and simmer for approximately 2 minutes till sauce thickens. Then add fresh basil and Parmigiano Reggiano cheese. Simultaneously, cook pasta, and in a bowl add sauce to pasta and toss.

Note: Also Boletus Brisa. This well known variety grows mainly in the Appennino Emiliano around Parma, in Valtellina, in the Appennino Toscano around Garfagnana, Piemonte hills, Sila and Pollina in Calabria, but they can also be found in other mountain areas. The best are the porcini picked in chestnut woods. They have a light-colored hat and a butter-white under hat. Porcini with dark hats are from the beech or fir tree and are more suitable to be preserved. They can be eaten as a salad or can be braised, cooked in a sauce, grilled or sautéed. They are also preserved in oil or dried for commercial consumption.

MINESTRA DI ZUCCHINE E SCALOGNO

Country Soup of Zucchini and Leeks

Yield: 6 servings

Ingredients

2 tablespoons	extra virgin olive oil
1 tablespoon	unsalted butter
2 large	leeks, white part only, cut into 1/2" slices
1 medium	onion, thinly sliced
4	scallions, cut into 1/2" slices
2 cloves	garlic, minced
5 zucchini	unpeeled, cut into 1/2" slices
2 cups	white potatoes, peeled and cut into 1/4" slices
5 cups	chicken stock (fresh or canned)
1 tablespoon	lemon juice
1/2 teaspoon	salt
1/4 teaspoon	black pepper, freshly ground
1 teaspoon	each, marjoram, thyme, rosemary
2 teaspoons	Worcestershire sauce
1 cup	whipping cream, or more as needed
2 tablespoons	chopped chives for garnish

Preparation

Heat olive oil and unsalted butter in a 4 to 5-quart saucepan and sauté leeks, onion, scallions, garlic, zucchini and potatoes until slightly softened, 5 to 10 minutes, stirring frequently. Add chicken stock and lemon juice and bring to a boil. Add kosher salt and pepper and herbs. Simmer until vegetables are soft, about 25 minutes. Puree soup in blender or processor in several batches. Stir in Worcestershire sauce and cream. (if soup is too thick, add more cream.) Allow to cool, then refrigerate.

Serve cold, garnished with chives.

CONIGLIO ALLA MOLISANA

Rabbit with Sausages

Yield: 6 servings

Ingredients

1 large	rabbit (about 3 1/2 pounds)
	salt and pepper to taste
1/4 cup	fresh Italian parsley, finely chopped
1 sprig	rosemary, finely chopped
1/4 pound	Prosciutto, julienne
12 leaves	fresh sage
6 large	Italian sausages (mild)
1/2 cup	extra virgin olive oil

Preparation

Bone the rabbit carefully, keeping the pieces of meat as large as possible.

Wipe the rabbit meat with a damp cloth. Cut into 12 even pieces, flatten lightly, and season with salt, pepper and a little finely chopped parsley and rosemary. Put a slice of ham on each slice of rabbit and roll up tightly.

Arrange 6 skewers, thread a roll of rabbit, 1 fresh sage leaf, another rabbit roll and another fresh sage leaf, alternating to finish each 6 skewers. Brush the skewers with oil and broil (grill), over charcoal if possible, or on a rack placed as close as possible to the source of heat. Alternatively, the skewers can also be baked in a slow oven at 350° F. for one hour. Turn the skewers occasionally, each time brushing with oil.

Note: Can be substituted with duck, chicken or quail.

CONIGLIO ALLA MOLISANA

Molise is a region of Italy north of Campania, south of Abruzzo. Its historic and political connection to Abruzzo ended when Molise became an independent region in 1963, but still shares some of the culinary traditions of its cousins. Their dialects are influenced by the relocation of Apoundanian speaking people who have migrated there for centuries.

COSTOLETTE FARCITE

Stuffed Veal Chops

Yield: 6 servings

Ingredients

1/2 pound	Fontina cheese (found in gourmet shops)
6	(1" thick) veal chops (from your butcher)
	salt and pepper to taste
2 1/2 tablespoons	all-purpose flour
1 large	egg, well beaten
1/2 cup	fine, dry breadcrumbs
6 tablespoons	unsalted butter
3 small	lemons, cut in wedges
	parsley sprigs (optional)

Preparation

Slice the cheese thinly. Cut a slit into the side of each veal chop to form a pocket.

Stuff the pockets with the cheese. Place the chops on a flat surface and press the top and bottom together. Seal the edges by beating hard with a heavy knife or mallet. Season lightly with the kosher salt and pepper. Dredge the chops in the flour, dip in the beaten egg, and coat with the breadcrumbs. Melt the unsalted butter in a heavy skillet or sauté pan.

Add the chops and sauté about 15 minutes or until golden brown on both sides. Serve piping hot, surrounded by the lemon wedges and garnished, if desired, with a few parsley sprigs.

Serve with a good Polenta.

COSTOLETTE FARCITE

The most famous of Cotolette is 'alla Milanese' from the city of Milan, fried in butter and served with lemon. It is believed to be a dish brought into Italy by the Austrians who ruled Lombardia for two centuries. I think the Austrians copied the dish from us.

MIGLIACCI DI TUNNARA

Crepes with Tuna

Yield: 6 servings

Ingredients

1 can (6 1/2 oz.)	tuna, packed in olive oil
1 can (2 oz.)	anchovies, chopped
1 tablespoon	fresh Italian parsley, chopped
	salt and freshly ground black pepper
1/2 cup	all-purpose flour
1/2 cup	cold water
3 eggs	slightly beaten
1 teaspoon	salt
2 tablespoons	extra virgin olive oil, brushing

MIGLIACCI DI TUNNARA

Migliaccio is a baked cake or pudding made with blood pudding or chestnut flour. Migliaccio Napoletano is a sformato made by alternating polenta with blood sausages and fresh mozzarella, usually made in January.

Preparation

Drain oil from tuna and anchovies and finely chop the fish. Add parsley, kosher salt and pepper to taste, and mix well. Beat the flour with half the water to avoid forming lumps. Add remaining water and mix well. Add eggs, onion kosher salt and 1/4 teaspoon pepper and beat well.

Heat a 4 inch skillet; brush bottom with oil. Pour 2 or 2 1/2 tablespoons of unsalted butter in skillet, tilting to spread the crepe evenly. Cook 3 minutes or until bottom is done but the top is still somewhat moist. Place 1 tablespoon of tuna mixture off center on edges; fold other edge on top; with a fork seal the open semicircular edge.

Turn Migliaccini onto ungreased baking sheet, as you make them. Then bake in 450° F. oven for 5 to 6 minutes.

Serve hot.

COSTOLETTA ALLA PIZZAIOLA

Veal Chop Pizzaiola Style

Yield: 4 servings

Ingredients

4 - 1 inch thick	veal T-bone loin chops
2 teaspoons	extra virgin olive oil
2 teaspoons	oregano, dried, crumbled
	salt and freshly ground black pepper
4 teaspoons	extra virgin olive oil
1 medium	onion, finely minced
1 can	Italian plum tomatoes with fresh basil, drained and chopped (reserve juice)
2 large	garlic cloves, flattened
1 teaspoon	sugar, granulated
1 teaspoon	basil, dried, crumbled
1 teaspoon	oregano, dried crumbled
8	anchovy fillets, pounded to smooth paste
4 teaspoons	capers, drained for garnish
	fresh Italian parsley, minced

Preparation

Pat veal chops dry; rub with oil, oregano, salt, and pepper. Arrange in single layer in baking dish. Set aside at room temperature for 2 hours. Heat oil in heavy (or non-stick), large skillet over medium heat. Add onion and cook until wilted. Stir in chopped tomatoes, garlic, sugar, fresh basil, and oregano. Increase heat to medium-high; cook until juice evaporates,

COSTOLETTA ALLA PIZZAIOLA

Definitely a sauce of Neapolitan origin, it is so called because it resembles the seasoned tomato topping for pizza with plenty of tomato, spiced with oregano.

about 5 minutes. Blend in reserved tomato juice with anchovy fillets. Partially cover and cook until thickened, about 10 minutes. Stir in capers and cook for 5 minutes longer. Grease broiler pan and position about 3" from heat; preheat pan and broiler. Transfer chops to heated pan; cook, turning several times, until charred and crusty on outside and juicy inside, about 10 minutes total. Transfer chops to individual plates (warmed). Top evenly with sauce. Sprinkle with parsley and serve hot.

Crout Street which ran off of Spruce Street. This was one of the first areas of pushcarts and horse drawn wagons. Mornings would be filled with fruit and vegetables and the vendor would circulate this territory with his goods. These fruit stands later moved to both sides of Spruce Street and in early thirties, they again moved to permanent stands on Arthur Avenue, which later became Balbo Avenue and today De Pasquale Avenue. Circa 1928.

CROSTINI DI FUNGHI MISTI

Mushroom Crostini

Yield: 12 servings

Ingredients

1 ounce	imported dried Porcini mushrooms
3 tablespoons	extra virgin olive oil
1 tablespoon	unsalted butter
1/2 pound	fresh shiitake, sliced
1/4 cup	heavy cream
2 tablespoons	fresh Italian parsley, minced
3 tablespoons	Asiago or Parmigiano Reggiano cheese, grated
8 large	Italian bread, lightly toasted

Preparation

Soak porcini in 1cup very hot water for 20 minutes. Drain and dice, removing any hard stem pieces. (Strain and save the liquid to use in soup.)

Heat oil and unsalted butter in a large skillet until unsalted butter foams. Add mushrooms and cook until lightly golden. Add garlic and cook and stir for one minute.

Add cream and cook until slightly thickened, about 5 minutes. Add parsley and stir briefly. Season to taste with salt and a couple of grinds of black pepper.

Cool slightly (can be made ahead) and mound on toasts. Sprinkle with cheese and run under a preheated broiler until cheese is melted and all is bubbly and beginning to brown.

Serve immediately.

CROSTINI DI FUNGHI MISTI

Crostini are thin slices of toast topped with various ingredients, such as chicken liver as in Tuscany. In Rome bone marrow is applied to the top. Crostino is different from bruschetta and is generally served as antipasto or merenda (snack).

CROSTINI DI POLENTA AI FUNGHI

Mushrooms and Polenta Crostini

Yield: 8 servings

Ingredients

1 ounce	porcini mushrooms, dried
4 tablespoons	extra virgin olive oil
1	large red onion, finely minced
1 pound	fresh white mushrooms, cleaned and sliced
3	small ripe plum tomatoes, chopped
1 tablespoon	fresh parsley, minced
	salt and black pepper to taste

Polenta

6 cups	water
2 1/2 teaspoons	salt
2 cups	cornmeal, finely ground
	extra virgin olive oil, for brushing

Preparation

Soak the porcini mushrooms in warm water to cover for at least 45 minutes. Carefully remove from liquid and rinse well under cold water. Chop roughly and pat dry. Heat olive oil in a heavy sauté pot and sauté onion until it is translucent and soft. Add the garlic and all the mushrooms. Reduce heat to low and cook, stirring intermittently, for 20 to 25 minutes, until tender. Add the tomatoes, parsley, kosher salt and black pepper and cook for another 5 minutes.

Polenta: Bring the salted water to vigorous boil in a large pot. Reduce heat to low and slowly sprinkle in the cornmeal in a thin stream, first whisking in, then stirring constantly to avoid any lumps. Keep the water at a steady simmer and stir frequently. When it comes away from the side of the pot, after 20 or 25 minutes, then it is cooked. Check for salt. Allow to cool before pouring onto a baking sheet and patting until it is as smooth as possible. Cut the polenta into slices that are 2" wide and 3" to 4" long. Brush lightly with the olive oil. Broil until they are firm and lightly crisp on both sides. Place a spoonful of the hot mushroom sauce on the top of each crostini and serve.

FOCACCIA AL FINOCCHIO

Fennel Focaccia

Yield: 12 slices

Ingredients

2 pounds	frozen bread dough
1/2 cup	extra virgin olive oil
	corn meal
2 teaspoons	salt
1 teaspoon	black pepper, freshly ground
2 teaspoons	fennel seeds

Preparation

Heat oven to 475° F. Divide dough in half. Spread 2 tablespoons oil in each of two 10" x 15" cookie pans (with sides) and sprinkle with cornmeal. Press dough into pans and tap surface with your fingers for a dimpled top.

Drizzle remaining oil over dough. Combine salt, pepper and fennel seeds. Sprinkle over the dough.

Rest in a non - ventilated area for 30 minutes (The dough will lightly rise.)

Bake until golden brown, about 10 minutes. Cut into wedges and serve warm or at room temperature.

Note: Serve this Focaccia with fresh fennel on the top, thinly sliced and previously tossed in olive oil.

FOCACCIA AL FINOCCHIO

Focaccia is a dimpled yeast bread thicker than pizza. From the Latin focus (hearth), it is believed to be a Ligurian invention but is made throughout Italy with many different toppings. In Apulia, tomatoes, garlic, and olive oil are placed in the indentations of the dough before baking. This is called Puddica.

CRESCIA

Focaccia Marchigiana

Yield: 1 Focaccia (12 slices)

Ingredients

2 1/2 teaspoons	dried yeast
1/2 cup	warm water
1 1/2 cups	water, room temperature
6 tablespoons	extra virgin olive oil
5 cups	unbleached all-purpose flour
1 tablespoon	salt

Topping

2 tablespoons	extra virgin olive oil
1 cup	onions, finely chopped
1 1/2 tablespoons	extra virgin olive oil
1/2 teaspoon	salt

CRESCIA

Although found in the Marche region, this specialty was created in the city of Gubbio in Umbria, believed to be a favorite of the Duke of Montofeltro.

Preparation

Stir the yeast into a small bowl and let proof for 10 minutes. Stir in the rest of the water and oil. Whisk in 2 cups of the flour and stir till smooth. Add salt and the rest of the flour, 1 cup at a time. Knead for 8 to 10 minutes until soft and velvety. Place in a lightly oiled bowl, cover and let rise until doubled. While the dough is rising, prepare the topping. Warm the olive oil over low heat and sauté the onions for about 20 minutes. Cool to room temperature. Cut the dough into 2 pieces, one twice as large as the other. Shape the smaller one to fit an oiled 10" round pie plate and the larger one to fit an oiled 10 1/2" X 15 1/2" baking sheet. Cover and let rise for 45 minutes until bubbles appear in the dough but it has not quite doubled. Heat the oven to 400° F. for 30 minutes before baking. Sprinkle the onions over the dough and drizzle with olive oil and finish with the salt. Bake for 25 minutes until the onions are golden. Cool on wire racks and serve as an appetizer or snack.

Variation: Crescia al Rosmarino. Substitute 2 tablespoons finely chopped rosemary for the onions.

FOCACCIA PUGLIESE

Focaccia from Puglia

Yield: 2 focacce

Ingredients

Dough:

8 ounces	potatoes (1 large)
1 1/4 teaspoons	dried yeast
1 1/2 cups	warm water
3 3/4 cups	all-purpose flour
2 teaspoons	salt

Topping:

3 tablespoons	extra virgin olive oil
1 large	ripe tomato, seeded and cubed
2 teaspoons	capers, rinsed
1/2 teaspoon	salt
1/2 teaspoon	oregano, dried

Preparation

About 20 minutes before making the dough, peel potatoes and boil them until tender. Drain and mash them. Use potatoes while they are still warm.

Stir yeast into the warm water in a large mixing bowl. Add flour, potatoes and salt in two additions. Mix together.

Knead for 10 minutes. Place dough in a lightly oiled bowl, cover and let rise until doubled. Divide dough in half and shape into a ball. Place each ball into a well-oiled 9" round baking pan and stretch the dough towards the edges.

Cover, let sit for10 minutes, then stretch a little more. Cover again and set aside until doubled. Preheat oven to 400° F. Dimple dough with your finger. Sprinkle with olive oil, spread with tomatoes, capers, salt and oregano.

Bake for 25 to 30 minutes until golden. Cool on wire racks. Serve and eat at room temperature.

CUCUZZARA

Squash Bread

Yield: 8 loaves

Ingredients

3/4 cup	extra virgin olive oil
1 medium	onion, thinly sliced
2/3 pound	butternut squash, peeled and diced
1	red pepper, roasted and cut into strips
4 ounces	tomatoes, peeled, seeded and diced
1 1/2 teaspoons	dried yeast
1 1/2 cups	warm water
13-16 cups	durum flour biga
7 cups	durum flour
1 tablespoon	salt
	red pepper flakes (optional)

CUCUZZARA

Cucuzza a term used in Puglia for squash. My friend Cosimo Della Torre prepares a wonderul Biga with flour, yeast and water.

Preparation

About 1 hour before you are ready to make the bread, warm 1/4 cup olive oil in a skillet and sauté the onions over medium-low heat until they are soft but still slightly crunchy. Add the squash and pepper. Cover and cook for 20 minutes. Add the tomatoes and cook another 3 to 5 minutes. Cool.

Stir the yeast into the water and let proof for 10 minutes. Add the biga and mix well. Add the reserved olive oil. Stir in the cooked vegetables. Add the flour and salt slowly, mixing until the dough comes together.

Knead with wet hands until the dough is firm, velvety and elastic. Place dough in an oiled bowl, cover and let rise until doubled, about 3 hours.

Divide dough into 8 pieces and shape into long cylinders.

Place on floured baking sheets, cover and let rise until well doubled, about an hour. Preheat the oven to 400° F. Bake for 35 to 45 minutes, until golden. Serve warm.

FRITTATA DI CAMPAGNA CON FONTINA

Country Style Frittata

Yield: 4 servings

Ingredients

8 large	eggs
6 ounces	Fontina cheese, cubed
1/3 cup	onions, finely chopped
1/3 cup	green peppers, chopped
1/4 cup	parsley, finely chopped
	salt
	freshly ground black pepper
	extra virgin olive oil

FRITTATA DI CAMPAGNA CON FONTINA

Frittata is a preparation of eggs and other ingredients. Sometimes it's a clever way of using up leftovers, especially vegetables. Its name derives from the Latin 'frigere', to fry.

Preparation

Grill green peppers then peel and julienne.

In a skillet, sauté onion in oil until transparent, set aside until needed. In a bowl, beat eggs until frothy, then add green peppers, salt, pepper and onions. In the same skillet (adding more oil if necessary), cook the omelette on both sides until still a little soft inside (alla lacrima, or runny "like a teardrop"), but well-cooked on the outside. Set omelette on an oven plate and top with cheese. Bake in oven preheated to 300° F. until Fontina has melted.

Sprinkle with parsley and serve immediately.

Note: Fontina is an ancient cheese from Valle D'Aosta. Mild and semi-soft, it is made from cow's milk, and aged for four months. Fontal is a variety from Trentino similar to Fontina used for cooking.

FETTUCCINE ALLA ROMANA

Roman-Style Fettuccine

Yield: 4 servings

Ingredients

1/2 pound	unsalted butter, softened
1 large	egg yolk
1/4 cup	heavy cream
1/2 cup	Parmigiano Reggiano cheese, freshly grated
1 tablespoon	salt
1 pound	fresh fettuccine
	salt and black pepper to taste

Preparation

Beat unsalted butter until light and fluffy.

Slowly add the egg yolk and cream, beating constantly.

Add grated cheese, a few tablespoons at a time, beating after each addition.

In a large pan, bring approximately 8 quarts of water to boil; add salt and very gently drop in the fettuccine. Stir with a wooden spoon for a few moments to separate the noodles, and cook for about 7 minutes, or until tender. The pasta should be al dente, or firm to the bite.

Drain the fettuccine into a colander and place in a large heated serving bowl. Add the creamed unsalted butter and cheese immediately; toss very gently and season generously with salt and pepper. Serve immediately.

FETTUCCINE ALLA ROMANA

A very rich interpretation of the classic Fettuccine Alfredo, which originated in Rome at the beginning of the Century to become one of the most emblematic representations of Cucina Italiana in the world.

FILETTO DI BUE ARRICCHITO

Rich Beef Filet

Yield: 4 servings

Ingredients

4 - 4 ounces each	filets of beef
1/4 teaspoon	salt
	freshly ground black pepper
1 clove	garlic, minced
8 slices	Prosciutto ham
4 medium slices	mozzarella cheese
2 tablespoons	truffles or white mushrooms, thinly sliced
1 teaspoon	fresh Italian parsley, chopped
1 tablespoon	Romano cheese, grated
3 medium	eggs, beaten
1/4 cup	milk, whole
3/4 cup	fine breadcrumbs
3 tablespoons	clarified unsalted butter
2 tablespoons	extra virgin olive oil
	juice of 1 lemon
1/4 cup	white wine, dry
1/4 cup	fresh or canned chicken broth
	watercress or endive sprigs for garnish

FILETTO DI BUE ARRICCHITO

The diversity in the preparation of beef in Italian cooking is nearly endless. Regardless of the recipe, it should be noted that herbs and spices are only used to highlight the basic taste of meat. Gabriele D'Annunzio (1863-1938), a dramatist, novelist and flamboyant political leader, was also a noted gourmand. He would peek in the kitchen of his mansion and constantly remind his cooks of one thing: "Non dimenticate, I sapori, I sapori", that is, "do whatever you wish to the food but don't forget the basic flavors".

Preparation

Preheat oven to 375° F.

Horizontally slice each filet butterfly-style leaving edge intact so filet is not completely cut through. Season with salt, pepper and garlic. In center of each filet place 2 slices Prosciutto, one slice mozzarella and several slices of truffle or mushrooms. Close halves of each filet like a sandwich. Press meat together around edges to seal. Beat parsley and grated cheese into eggs.

Dip meat into milk, then into breadcrumbs, and finally into eggs. Heat unsalted butter and oil in sauté pan until bubbling hot. Add filets and cook over low heat until nicely browned on both sides.

Drain off cooking fat. Add lemon juice, wine and chicken stock to skillet and place in pre-heated oven for approximately 10 minutes (less time is required for rare, longer for well-done).

Pour a little pan juice over each filet, then garnish with sprigs of watercress or endive and serve hot.

A Sunday Feast Day Procession. A band leading the Mutual Aid Society Members of Holy Ghost Church up Atwells Avenue. These Sunday Feast Day Processions were very popular, as all the participants planned one year ahead for this occasion. They began as Mutual Benefit Societies with small numbers. The societies grew and became a helpful force for obtaining doctors and death certificates for their members. Circa 1906.

FUNGHI RIPIENI CON LUMACHE

Mushrooms Filled with Snails

Yield: 4 servings

Ingredients

24 medium sized	fresh mushrooms, washed, dried, stems removed
3/4 pound	unsalted butter, softened
24	escargot, canned
2 tablespoons	white wine (dry)
	salt and black pepper to taste
3 cloves	garlic, peeled
1 tablespoon	fresh lemon juice
2 tablespoons	fresh parsley, minced

Preparation

Preheat oven to 350° F. Sauté mushroom caps in 4 tablespoons of unsalted butter for 3 to 4 minutes on each side or until golden brown. Set aside. Sauté escargots in white wine and 4 tablespoons unsalted butter for 10 minutes. Salt and pepper to taste. Drain.

Fill each mushroom cap with a snail. Place remaining unsalted butter, garlic, and lemon juice in a blender and make a paste. Place a lump of paste on each mushroom and bake 10 minutes on a baking sheet. Sprinkle with parsley. Brown under broiler and serve hot.

FUNGHI RIPIENI CON LUMACHE

Mushrooms and truffles belong to the same vegetable family (funghi); the main difference is that mushrooms grow on the surface, receiving their nourishment from the earth, whereas truffles grow underground, feeding themselves through the roots of trees.

GNOCCHI ALLO ZAFFERANO

Gnocchi with Saffron

Yield: 4 servings

Ingredients

1 pound	semolina flour
1/4 cup	extra virgin olive oil
1 large	onion, chopped
1/4 cup	fresh Italian parsley, chopped
1/2 teaspoon	saffron (available in specialty shops)
3 ounces	pork fat, chopped
7 ounces	ground pork
7 ounces	lamb, lean, ground
1 1/2 pounds	tomatoes, chopped fine in food processor
2	bay leaves
6	fresh sage leaves, or 1/2 teaspoon dried
	salt and black pepper to taste
3/4 cup	Pecorino cheese, grated (optional)

Preparation

To make Gnocchi:

Pour flour onto work surface and make a well in the center. Pour in olive oil. Dissolve saffron in a bit of warm water and add to well. Mix liquid with flour, adding enough water to form a firm, not sticky, dough.

Add water 1/4 cup at a time, until dough is the right consistency. Cut dough into pieces and roll into long cylinders, about 1/2" diameter. Cut into 1" chunks and press your finger into each gnocchi to make a deep dent.

Set gnocchi aside on a floured surface to dry while you make the sauce. Heat pork fat in sauté pan and cook the onion and parsley until tender. Stir in the ground meat and cook until no longer pink. Add the chopped tomatoes, bay leaves, kosher salt and pepper.

Cook, uncovered, for an hour or until the sauce is thickened. Cook gnocchi in boiling salted water until al dente. Drain and arrange in pasta dishes. Pour sauce over top and garnish with a handful of grated cheese.

ORECCHIETTE DI CASA

Homemade Orecchiette

Yield: 4 servings (1 1/2 pounds of fresh pasta)

Ingredients

1 cup	semolina flour
2 cups	unbleached all-purpose flour
1/4 teaspoon	salt
3/4 cup, approx.	lukewarm water

Preparation

Combine semolina, unbleached flour and salt, and mound on a large work surface. Make a well in the center with your finger and pour in 3 - 4 Tbls. water. Begin pulling flour from the inner wall of the well into the liquid. Add more water and continue forming a paste until flour has absorbed as much water as possible without becoming hard or dry. (The perfect consistency is softer than basic flour- and- egg pasta, but not at all sticky). Knead vigorously on a lightly floured board until dough is smooth and elastic. This may take 20 minutes or so. Form dough into a ball and cover.

To make the 'little ears', pull off a scant handful of the dough (keep the rest of the dough covered). On a lightly floured board, roll the dough into a rope about 3/4" in diameter. Cut the rope into slices no more than 1/8 inch thick to form small circles of dough. Now put circle into the cupped palm of your hand and, with the thumb of the other hand, press and turn the circle at the

ORECCHIETTE DI CASA

A pasta shape that resembles small human ears from the region of Puglia are generally cooked with Broccoli di rape with the addition of anchovies and hot peperoncino. La Signora Giuseppina Lomartire make these wonderful orecchiette on weekends for her family.

same time to form a dent in the center that will spread the dough a little on each side. It should look like a small ear, with slightly thicker earlobes. Repeat with remaining dough, placing the orecchiette on a lightly floured cloth when shaped.

Orecchiette are cooked in the same manner as fresh flour-and -egg pasta, although they take longer to cook. Watch them carefully and taste frequently for al dente.

Jimmy Pandozzi, reading in front of his son's fruit store on Spruce Street. This was one of the larger fruit and vegetable stores on Federal Hill, where an abundance of fresh fruit and vegetables could be purchased daily. Circa 1936.

GNOCCHI DI SEMOLINA

Roman Gnocchi

Yield: 4 servings

Ingredients

3 1/2 cups	milk, whole
3/4 cup	fine semolina
1/2 cup	unsalted butter
6 tablespoons	Parmigiano Reggiano cheese, grated
2 large	egg yolks
	salt and black pepper to taste
	pinch of ground nutmeg
	breadcrumbs

Preparation

Heat milk with a pinch of salt, and when it boils gradually add semolina, stirring constantly with a wooden spoon to avoid lumps. Continue to cook, stirring, for 20 minutes. Remove from heat and add 2 tablespoons unsalted butter in small pieces, gradually stir in 2 tablespoons Parmigiano Reggiano cheese, the egg yolks, one at a time, a pinch of pepper and nutmeg. Oil 1 or 2 large dishes or clean marble kitchen slab and pour semolina mixture on. Spread to 1/2" thickness using a cold wet spatula and allow to cool.

Preheat oven to 350° F. Melt remaining 6 tablespoons unsalted butter; reserving some for serving. Cut out squares or circles of semolina dough and place in greased dish. Drizzle with unsalted butter and sprinkle with Parmigiano Reggiano, add a layer of gnocchi, and repeat. Sprinkle breadcrumbs over gnocchi and bake for about 20 minutes or until golden brown. Serve hot.

They said;
I had to chisel the ice in the sink with an ice pick,
so that I could wash up in the morning. And I was not the only one.

FUSILLI ALLA SORRENTINA

Sorrento Style Pasta

Yield: 4 servings

Ingredients

1 1/2 pounds	fusilli, cooked al dente
5 ounces	tuna, canned in olive oil
4 ripe	tomatoes, fresh, cubed
1/4 cup	black olives, pitted and chopped
	extra virgin olive oil
	salt
	freshly ground black pepper
2 large	cloves garlic, finely chopped
	fresh Italian parsley, minced
6	mint leaves, fresh
1/4 cup	white wine, dry

Preparation

Drain the tuna. In a skillet, sauté the garlic and parsley in a little oil over medium heat. As soon as the garlic starts to become transparent, add tuna, crumbled and cook for 2 minutes. Add olives, wine and tomatoes, and simmer for 10 to 15 minutes longer. Add mint leaves, salt and pepper. Toss in the cooked pasta and mix gently.

Serve immediately.

Note: Cereals have always been the primary dietary source of people throughout the ages. In Italy, the daily diet, since ancient Rome, consisted mostly of pultes (flours) made of ground barley, rye or farro.

FUSILLI ALLA SORRENTINA

Fusilli is a pasta shaped like a corkscrew, sometimes called eliche (propellers). In the town of Acrl in Calabria, fusilli are called fischietti. In Piemonte a similar shaped pasta is called macaron de fret.

VITELLINA AL CHIANTI

Veal Escalopes with Chianti Wine

Yield: 4 servings

Ingredients

2 pounds	veal cutlets, sliced thin
	all-purpose flour
2 teaspoons	extra virgin olive oil
2 teaspoons	Prosciutto, diced
1/2 cup	unsalted butter
1 small	onion, peeled and diced
1/3 teaspoon	salt
1/3 teaspoon	freshly ground black pepper
1/4 cup	Chianti or Cabernet Sauvignon
1/2 pound	fresh mushrooms, (white or shiitake)
2 medium	green peppers, thinly sliced
2 large	tomatoes, thinly sliced
1 large clove	garlic, mashed
8 sprigs	fresh parsley, leaves only

VITELLINA AL CHIANTI

I particularly enjoy the taste of the Sangiovese grape in the Chianti wine, but a crisp and robust Cabernet may also be used for this preparation.

Preparation

Pound cutlets thin and sprinkle with flour on both sides, shaking excess. Place olive oil, Prosciutto and unsalted butter in a skillet to heat. Add onions and sauté until medium brown. Add veal and brown slowly for 3 minutes. Turn, and cook for 2 minutes. Add salt, pepper and wine. Cover and simmer for 5 minutes. Separate stems and caps of mushrooms. Chop stems finely and caps into thin slices. Discard cores and seeds from peppers and cut into very thin slices. Add mushrooms, green peppers and tomatoes to veal, cover, and cook for 5 minutes. Chop garlic and parsley together and stir the mixture into the sauce.

Simmer uncovered for 10 minutes; serve hot.

INSALATA DI FAVA

Fava Bean Salad

Yield: 4 servings

Ingredients

8 ounces	dried fava beans, soaked, or 3 pounds fresh
1 large	onion, quartered
1 1/4 teaspoons	salt
2 teaspoons	lemon juice
2 tablespoons	extra virgin olive oil
1 1/2 tablespoons	fresh Italian parsley, chopped
1/2 teaspoon	salt
1/2 teaspoon	freshly ground black pepper
1 clove	garlic, minced

Preparation

Drain the beans and slip them out of their skins, by squeezing between thumb and index fingers. Set the skinned beans in a pot with the onion and just enough water to cover. Bring to a boil, over medium heat, add salt and reduce to a simmer. Cover and cook until the water has almost evaporated and the beans are tender and pulpy, 20 to 25 minutes. Drain the beans. Mix together the lemon juice, olive oil, parsley, salt and pepper. Toss with the garlic and the cooked beans.

Serve as an antipasto, or as we would serve a potato salad.

INSALATA DI FAVA

I remember cleaning favas with my grandfather, Michele Seconi. He had lived in Virginia for 40 years, and upon his return to Italy at age 70, he still managed to plant fava for the crop in April. As he smoked his pipe he would remark: "Questa e 'lussuria per I poveri": This is the luxury of the poor.
Fava beans derive from the Latin faba, named after an aristocratic family, the Fabii. Young fresh fava is often eaten raw accompanied by aged Pecorino cheese, and is also wonderful in soups such as Favata from Sardinia.

AVVOLTO DI PROSCIUTTO ED ASPARAGI

Bundles of Prosciutto & Asparagus

Yield: 4 servings

Ingredients

12 thick stalks or 24 thin	asparagus, trimmed
6 tablespoons	unsalted butter
6 slices	Prosciutto, halved crosswise
1/2 cup	all-purpose flour, for dredging
2 large	eggs
1 tablespoon	vegetable oil

AVVOLTO DI PROSCIUTTO ED ASPARAGI

Prosciutto is made by salting, aging and dressing a pork leg, then preparing it according to local usage. The Parma Prosciutto is cut with a short shank or "like a chicken leg" as the natives say. The San Daniele has the leg flattened so that it remains much stiffer. It is salted and placed under weight, a method that allows the leg to discard more moisture.

Preparation

Fill a large, high-sided skillet with salted water and bring to a boil. Add the asparagus and cook until just tender, about 10 minutes. Drain in a colander, refresh under cold water and drain again. Pat dry and spread on a platter.

In a small saucepan, melt 3 tablespoons of the unsalted butter. Drizzle it over the asparagus. Wrap 1 piece of Prosciutto around the middle of 1 thick or 2 thin asparagus stalks.

Place the flour on a plate. Beat the eggs in a wide shallow bowl. Roll one of the asparagus bundles in the flour, then dip in the egg and return to the platter. Repeat with the remaining bundles.

In a large skillet, heat the remaining 3 tablespoons unsalted butter and the oil over moderate heat. Working in batches, add the asparagus bundles and fry, turning once, until golden, about 4 minutes.

Drain on paper towels; serve at once.

Easter time on Federal Hill. Shown is Pasquale Di Giulio. A common scene on Federal Hill at Easter time. This photo was taken on Spruce Street in 1932.

SPAGHETTI E VONGOLE

Pasta with Red Clam Sauce

Yield: 6 servings

Ingredients

4 pounds	clams (not too large)
1 tablespoon	salt (for soaking clams)
1/4 cup	extra virgin olive oil
6 large	cloves garlic, peeled and minced
1/4 teaspoon	red pepper flakes
10 3/4 ounces	tomato puree (1 can)
2/3 cup	dry white wine
1/2 cup	fresh Italian parsley, chopped
1 pound	spaghetti, cooked al dente (firm to the bite)

Preparation

Put clams into large pan and cover with cold water. Pour in the salt, stir, and refrigerate 30 minutes.

Heat olive oil over medium heat in a large pan. Add garlic and red pepper flakes; sauté about 2 minutes. Add tomato puree and wine. Boil. Reduce heat and simmer 5 minutes.

Drain clams in a colander and rinse well. Put clams into the sauce with half of the parsley. Bring to a boil, reduce heat to medium, cover and cook about 7 minutes or until clamshells have opened. Discard any clams not opened. Remove with slotted spoon, place in bowl, and cover with foil.

Drain pasta and put into the sauce. Stir for about 3 minutes so that pasta absorbs some of the sauce. Toss with the remaining parsley and clams. Serve on heated plates or in pasta bowls.

SPAGHETTI E VONGOLE

Vongola is a marine bivalve, but unlike mussels, their shells are light grey in color. As with all shellfish, clams must be cooked alive. In Rhode Island they are called "littlenecks".

VITELLINA AL LIMONE

Veal with Lemon Sauce

Yield: 4 servings

Ingredients

8	veal scallopine
1/4 cup	all-purpose flour
1 large	egg, beaten
2 tablespoons	milk, whole
6 tablespoons	unsalted butter
	salt and black pepper to taste
1	lemon, juice only
1	lemon, cut into 8 thin slices
1 tablespoon	fresh Italian parsley, finely chopped

Preparation

Pound the scaloppine lightly with a flat mallet. Sprinkle with salt and pepper and dust both sides in flour. Beat egg well with milk, salt, and pepper.

Dip veal in egg to coat on both sides. Heat butter in heavy skillet and add veal. Cook about 2 minutes on one side, or until golden. Turn and cook on other side until golden. Remove veal and add lemon juice to skillet. Reduce for 1 minute; pour over the veal.

Garnish with lemon slices and sprinkle with parsley. Serve hot.

VITELLINA AL LIMONE

The term "veal" is used in Italy to refer to the meat of both the male and the female calf. Calves are butchered from ages one month to one year old. If the calf has been raised on proper food (milk and selected fodder), both its meat and fat will be very white.

RISOTTO CON LE QUAGLIE

Risotto with Quail

Yield: 4 servings

Ingredients

	salt and ground black pepper
6 quails	boneless, prepared for cooking
4 leaves	fresh sage, whole
4 thin slices	lard or Pancetta (cured pork belly)
3 ounces	unsalted butter
2 tablespoons	brandy
1 cup	dry white wine
1 quart	beef broth, fresh or canned
1 medium	white onion, minced
10 ounces	long grain rice (Arborio or Carnaroli)
6 tablespoons	Parmigiano Reggiano, grated

Preparation

Salt and pepper the insides of quail and insert a fresh sage leaf. Wrap the quail with the Pancetta or lard slices, fastening with toothpicks. Melt 1 ounce butter in a saucepan and brown the quail, moistening with 1/2 cup of wine and brandy. When the wine evaporates, sprinkle with salt and pepper and roast for 12 minutes, moistening with broth as needed. Cool the quail, strain, de-glaze the pan juices and set aside. Quarter quail and remove breastbone. Return pan juices to the saucepan and add the quail pieces. Finish for another 6 minutes on moderate flame.

Meanwhile, prepare a risotto using half the remaining unsalted butter, the finely minced onion, the remaining wine, and the broth, in stages, while stirring with a wooden spoon. When the risotto is cooked al dente (about 18 minutes), remove from fire, add the remaining butter and Parmigiano Reggiano. Pour the risotto into a serving dish, arrange the quails in dish, alternating legs and breasts, and drizzle the border of the risotto with the pan juices to serve.

TRIPPA ALLA FIORENTINA

Tripe Firenze Style

Yield: 8 servings

Ingredients

2 pounds	tripe (cleaned and trimmed)
4 tablespoons	vegetable oil
2	carrots, grated
1/2 cup	celery, chopped
1 small	yellow onion, peeled and chopped
1/2 cup	fresh Italian parsley, chopped
3 cloves	garlic, crushed
1 (8 oz.)	can tomato sauce
1/2 cup	beef stock, fresh or canned
1/2 cup	dry red wine
1 teaspoon	oregano, dried
1	bay leaf, crushed
1/2 teaspoon	fresh basil, julienne
	salt and black pepper to taste
2 - 1" pieces	lemon peel
1/2 cup	Parmigiano Reggiano or Pecorino Romano cheese, freshly grated

TRIPPA ALLA FIORENTINA

Tripe is the stomach and the first parts of the intestine of cows, hogs and lamb, generally divided into four parts. On Federal Hill the second lining of cow's stomach is widely used, only if white and without excess fat surrounding the tissues.

Preparation

Parboil tripe for about 30 minutes. Drain and cool. Slice up tripe into 1/2" wide pieces. Sauté very quickly in a little of the oil in a large frying pan.

Sauté in half of the oil the carrots, celery, onion, parsley and garlic. Add tomato sauce, beef stock and wine. Add seasonings and lemon peel. Simmer the sauce for a few minutes, then add the tripe. Cook it on top of the stove, covered, for 1 1/2 hours or until tender, or bake it in a moderate oven, preferably in a Terra cotta pot for 1 hour at 300° F. When ready to serve, sprinkle with Parmigiano Reggiano or Romano. Serve with pasta, or mixed with cannellini beans.

SUPPLI AL TELEFONO

Rice Suppli

Yield: 4 servings

Ingredients

1 ounce	dried mushrooms
2 small	onions, finely chopped
4 ounces	unsalted butter
8 ounces	long grain rice (Arborio)
6 tablespoons	Parmigiano Reggiano, grated
	all-purpose flour
3 ounces	lean veal (ground)
	breadcrumbs
2 slices	Prosciutto, minced
	vegetable oil for frying
1 tablespoon	tomato paste.
4	ripe tomatoes, peeled, seeded and diced
	salt
1/4 pound	fresh mozzarella, diced
2 large	eggs, beaten

Preparation

Soak the mushrooms in lukewarm water, drain, chop and set aside. Sauté one onion in 2 ounces unsalted butter in a saucepan. When the onion is soft, add the rice and make a risotto as in basic recipe. Let risotto cool. Make a ragú by sautéeing one onion in remaining butter. When onions are soft, add veal, Prosciutto, and mushrooms. Add the tomato paste diluted in 1 cup warm water and salt; let simmer over a low flame. Let mixture cook and reduce to achieve a rather thick ragú. Remove from heat and cool. Take a small amount of rice in the palm of your hand, flatten, and place in the center a teaspoonful of the prepared ragú and a few pieces of mozzarella. Close your palm and form a ball. Make sure the filling is securely closed in the center of the ball. Roll the rice ball into flour, beaten egg and breadcrumbs, and continue until all the rice is finished. Fry the supplì in the hot oil until golden brown and crunchy.

FAGIOLI AL FIASCO

Beans Cooked in a Bottle

Yield: 8 servings

Ingredients

2/3 pound	cannellini beans, dried
	pinch of fresh rosemary
2 cloves	garlic
2 leaves	fresh sage, whole
8 ounces	olive oil, salt and pepper, mixed together

Preparation

Soak the beans in cold water overnight. Drain and place them in a flask-like container of flame-proof terracotta, together with garlic, fresh sage, rosemary, oil and 2 cups of water. Place the flask over the flame and let cook gently for 3 hours so that the water will evaporate and the beans absorb the oil. Place them in a tureen, add some more oil, pepper and salt.

Note: The cooking can be in a glass flask in a double boiler pot.

A photo of Atwells Avenue, the third building from the left is the restored building where today is located the Aqua Viva Euro Bristro. In the center of the photo, may be seen the Belfry of St. John Church, which was destroyed by fire.

POLENTA CON RAGÚ DI CARNE

Polenta & Meat Pasticcio

Yield: 4 servings

Ingredients

9 ounces	polenta flour (specialty shops)
1 1/2 quarts	water
4 tablespoons	unsalted butter
3 cups	meat ragú, or marinara
8 tablespoons	Parmigiano Reggiano, grated
1 ounce	white breadcrumbs
1 tablespoon	salt

Preparation

Preheat oven to 375° F. Prepare a polenta as in basic recipe. Pour into a large terracotta pot, previously moistened with water so sides do not stick. Cool. Turn the casserole upside down to unmold. With a long, wooden knife or a colorless string, cut the polenta horizontally in four equal layers. Butter the same baking dish, and pour in a few tablespoons of ragú. Layer polenta on the bottom, spread ragú over the layer of polenta and sprinkle with Parmigiano Reggiano. Repeat the operation with the remaining three layers of polenta in order to reconstruct its original form. Finish with the ragú, dot with unsalted butter and sprinkle with the remaining Parmigiano Reggiano mixed with a pinch of grated breadcrumbs.

Bake for about 40 minutes and serve hot.

POLENTA CON RAGÚ DI CARNE

Polenta is often served as a starch instead of bread, together with broiled cotechino, salami or cheese. I bake this polenta in terracotta pots such as my Tegamaccio. The intense flavor released from the clay is healthy and soothing.

PENNE D'ESTATE

Summertime Pasta

Yield: 6 servings

Ingredients

1 pound	penne or rigatoni
3 medium	zucchini
2 medium	onions
2 medium	fresh tomatoes
2	red apples, firm seeded, cored
1/2	sweet red pepper
6 2/3 tablespoons	extra-virgin olive oil
10 leaves	fresh basil
1 tablespoon	fresh Italian parsley, chopped
	salt and black pepper to taste

Preparation

Clean the zucchini, onions, tomatoes, apples and sweet pepper and cut into small cubes. Put the cubes in a blender and reduce to a puree, adding oil to obtain a creamy consistency. Season with salt and pepper; blend fresh basil and parsley with the puree. Pour the mixture into a large soup bowl. Cook the pasta until al dente. Set aside several tablespoons of the water, drain the penne and combine with the sauce, stirring in some of the water. Serve immediately.

PENNE D'ESTATE

Penne is part of the short pasta group, along with rigatoni, millerighe, sedani and maniche. These are all tubular in shape, varying in size and shape: straight, curved, smooth or grooved.

INSALATA DI TONNO E FAGIOLI

Tuna & Beans Salad

Yield: 4 servings

Ingredients

1 pound	cannellini beans, dried
6 ounce can	tuna in oil
1 medium	onion, thinly sliced
	salt
2 tablespoons	extra virgin olive oil
	pinch of black pepper

Preparation

Soak the beans overnight then cook for 1 1/2 hours, starting with cold salted water. Drain and cool. Combine in a bowl the beans, coarsely crumbled tuna and the onion. Add the olive oil, a pinch of black pepper and salt to taste. Toss well. Serve at room temperature.

Variation: The same recipe can be made with smoked herring instead of tuna. Cannellini beans can also be purchased canned (12 oz.).

INSALATA DI TONNO E FAGIOLI

Tuna can reach notable large dimensions, sometimes over 13 feet in length and up to 300 pounds. It has dark, compact flesh that may be a bit difficult to digest. The best part is the Ventresca, the underbelly part of the tuna. In this application canned tuna packed in olive oil will give you great results.

INSALATA DI POLIPETTI

Octopus Salad

Yield: 4 servings

Ingredients

3 pounds	baby octopus, cleaned and cubed
1 cup	extra virgin olive oil
1/4	fresh Italian parsley, minced
2 cloves	garlic, chopped
2 tablespoons	fresh lemon juice

Preparation

Clean the octopus well by turning inside out and removing eyes and the small bone at bottom of the head. Boil in a small amount of salted water for 25-45 minutes, according to size. Drain, peel, skin and cut octopus into small pieces. Transfer to a bowl. Season with chopped garlic, olive oil, lemon juice, salt, pepper and parsley. Let stand for a few hours before serving to allow octopus to become tender by absorbing the condiments.

Note: This salad is also excellent served immediately, while warm.

INSALATA DI POLIPETTI

Octopus is a sea creature found in many varietes. The polpo verace (stone octopus) can be identified by the double line of suckers on its tentacles. The octopus with red and white dots are known as scorria or polpessa.

BROCCOLETTI ALLA VITERBESE

Broccoli Viterbo Style

Yield: 4 servings

Ingredients

1 pound	broccoli di rabe, cleaned and washed
1	peperoncino (chile pepper)
2 tablespoons	extra virgin olive oil
	salt to taste
2 cloves	garlic, minced

Preparation

Wash the broccoli, removing the large stems and larger leaves.

Cook in salted boiling water for a few minutes, then drain and set aside.

In a large skillet, brown the garlic in the oil. Add the peperoncino and, when the garlic is brown, remove it and add the broccoli. Salt to taste and cook until tender but still crisp.

Note: Serve as a side dish to any white meat courses, such as fowl or pork.

Variations: Cooked broccoli di rabe can be pureed in food processor and tossed with a favorite pasta.

BROCCOLETTI ALLA VITERBESE

Very popular among southern Italians, this winter vegetable grows in bunches with slightly indented green leaves that have small green broccoli sprouts in the center.

INSALATA DI NERVETTI

Calf's Foot & Veal Shank Salad

Yield: 4 servings

Ingredients

1-2 pounds	veal shank (from your butcher)
1	calves' foot
1 large	onion, thinly sliced
1 large	carrot, thinly sliced
1 stalk	celery, thinly sliced
3 ounces	extra virgin olive oil
2 tablespoons	white vinegar
	salt and pepper to taste
1 tablespoon	fresh Italian parsley, chopped

Preparation

Clean veal shank and foot well, scraping and scorching them if necessary. Bring a large pot of salted water to a boil. Add carrot, celery, and half the onions. Add veal shank and foot: cook for about two hours or until meat begins to pull away from the bone. Drain. Let cool, then cut the meat into long, thin, equal strips.

Season with oil, vinegar, salt, black pepper and the remaining onion.

Top with chopped parsley and serve.

Note: Do not put the nervetti into the refrigerator or they will toughen. Keep them in a cool place.

INSALATA DI NERVETTI

A famous salad from the region of Lombardia. The name derives from the Latin "nervi", little nerves.

FRESELLA ALLA PUGLIESE

Fresella Apulian Style

Yield: 4 servings

Ingredients

3	freselle, from local Italian bakery
3	ripe tomatoes, peeled, seeded and coarsely chopped
	salt to taste
	pinch oregano
3 tablespoons	extra virgin olive oil

Preparation

Soften the whole freselle in water for 10 seconds and squeeze dry. Lay freselle on a plate and spread with a salad prepared with the tomatoes, oregano, salt, and extra virgin olive oil. (No pepper is necessary with this preparation because the frisedda has pepper in it).

FRESELLA ALLA PUGLIESE

Many Italo-Americans on the Hill are from Puglia, and this is one of their numerous gastronomic contributions.
Frisedda or Fresella is a ring-shaped roll made with whole wheat or white flour made in Apulia. It is twice baked to make it very crusty, then before eating is soaked in cold water and dressed to taste.

PUNTARELLE CON ACCIUGHE

Chicory with Anchovies

Yield: 4 servings

Ingredients

2 pounds	puntarelle
2 cloves	garlic, chopped
3	anchovy fillets, chopped
3 tablespoons	extra virgin olive oil
1	fresh lemon, squeezed
	salt and black pepper to taste

Preparation

Let the puntarelle soak in cold water for half an hour. Meanwhile blend the anchovies and garlic in a mortar until they become a paste. Blend in oil, lemon juice, a pinch of salt and pepper. Drain puntarelle, place them on a large bowl, toss with sauce, and serve.

Note: Serve in the summer topped with grilled chicken breast. Belgian endive may be a comparable substitute.

PUNTARELLE CON ACCIUGHE

Puntarelle is a Roman wild chicory. This very special salad is a specialty of Central Italy and only available in the winter months. Puntarelle must be washed and green leaves dispensed. The white-greenish tips are split with a knife lengthwise and dipped into cold water. This allows the leaves to curl and lose some of the bitter taste. Although puntarelle are not yet found commercially, immigrant Italians always have some in their gardens.

MAIALE AL LATTE

Pork Roast with Milk

Yield: 4 servings

Ingredients

2 pounds	leg of pork
4 cups	dry white wine
4 tablespoons	unsalted butter
	salt and black pepper to taste
4	sage leaves, fresh
2 sprigs	rosemary, fresh
1 quart	milk, whole

Preparation

Place the pork meat into a bowl, cover with wine and marinate for 4 hours in the refrigerator. Remove the pork from the marinade; dry it with kitchen towel. In a large roasting pan brown on all sides with the butter. Add salt, pepper, fresh sage leaves and rosemary, and cover with the milk. Cook slowly in oven at 375° F. for 1 hour, remove pork from casserole and set aside in a warm place. Reduce milk over high flame on top of the stove for 10 more minutes. Remove from heat and strain. Slice pork thin, arrange on serving platter, top with strained sauce, and serve.

Note: May be served with a Pamigiano Reggiano risotto, or polenta.

MAIALE AL LATTE

Coscia (leg) is a prime cut and it can be roasted when it is from a freshly killed pig. If the leg comes from a freshly killed young pig, it may also be braised, boiled or cooked in slices, when salted and air dried for several months becomes Prosciutto.

TRIGLIE ALLA LIVORNESE

Red Mullet Livorno Style

Yield: 4 servings

Ingredients

2 pounds	mullets, fresh
1 1/2 ounces	fresh Italian parsley, minced
1 stalk	celery, minced
2 cloves	garlic, minced
	salt and black pepper to taste
4 ounces	extra virgin olive oil
1 pound	ripe tomatoes, peeled, seeded and chopped
2 tablespoons	white flour, all-purpose

Preparation

Clean the mullet. In a large skillet, sauté parsley, celery and garlic with 2 ounce olive oil. When the vegetables are tender, add the tomatoes and cook for 10 minutes. Remove from heat and set aside. Coat the fish with flour; brown in a saucepan in oil until golden brown on both sides. Add salt and pepper to taste. Oil a terracotta casserole with oil, place mullet in it, and pour sauce into casserole to bake for 5 minutes at 450° F. Serve with a generous sprinkling of chopped parsley.

TRIGLIE ALLA LIVORNESE

Mullet is among the most expensive saltwater fish, despite its many thin bones. I call it the "woodcock of the sea" in that, like the woodcock, the red mullet can be eaten with its innards if fresh. In this case I grill it without washing it or removing the scales. There are two kinds of mullet: the red also called stone mullet, and white mullet. The profile of the red mullet is oblique whereas the white has a rosy color with silvery reflections on the sides.

PORCHETTA CONTADINA

Roast Suckling Pig

Yield: 24 servings

Ingredients

1	suckling pig 18-22 pounds
	extra virgin olive oil
2 tablespoons	dry white wine
1 tablespoon	wild fennel seeds
4 sprigs	rosemary, fresh
4 cloves	garlic, chopped
	salt and black pepper to taste
1 teaspoon each	coriander, nutmeg and peperoncino

Preparation

Chop and sauté the liver, heart and kidney in 2 tablespoons of olive oil. When hot, add the white wine to reduce and remove from heat. Season piglet with its own liver, heart and kidneys, plus wild fennel seeds, rosemary, salt, pepper, a good quantity of garlic, coriander, nutmeg, and peperoncino. Roll pig like a large sausage with fresh sage leaves, tie securely with colorless thread and roast whole for about 4 hours on a spit over charcoal made from aromatic wood. Cooking time varies according to the size of the piglet, which should be basted frequently with a rosemary sprig dipped in oil and with either white or red wine. The juice and fat that collects in the drip pan (leccarda) can be used to cook potatoes and onions, which may be served together with the porchetta.

Note: Porchetta can also be roasted in oven at 450° F. and basted every 30 minutes.

PORCHETTA CONTADINA

Porchetta is always boned to make it easier to serve and eat. It is a favorite among immigrant Italians especially during major celebrations such as Communions and birthdays.

PICCIONE RIPIENO

Stuffed Squab

Yield: 4 servings

Ingredients

4	squabs, about 2 pounds each
1/4 pound	top round of veal
1/4 pound	Pancetta
1/4 pound	Prosciutto, diced
1/4 pound	cooked pickled tongue, diced
1/4 pound	unsalted butter
1/2	onion, chopped
1/2	carrot, chopped
1/2 stalk	celery, chopped
2 cloves	garlic
4 ounces	Marsala wine
2 tablespoons	grated Parmigiano Reggiano
2	bay leaves
	salt and pepper to taste

PICCIONE RIPIENO

Squab are farm grown birds with delicate, lean meat. The best ones are those less than seven months old with tender, almost white meat. Older birds have tougher meat and must be cooked longer. If roasted, I usually wrap them with slices of Pancetta.

Preparation

Bone, wash and pat dry the squab. Grind the veal and the Pancetta and mix with the Prosciutto and tongue. Brown the vegetables in half of the butter, salt and pepper; add the ground and chopped meats, and cook for 15 minutes over medium heat. Add Marsala and Parmigiano Reggiano, mix well and remove from heat. Cool. Fill the squab with the stuffing and wrap with caul fat to prevent the stuffing from falling out. Place them in a terracotta pot or greased baking pan with the remaining unsalted butter, bay leaves and salt. Cook at 450° F. in oven for about 45 minutes, turning frequently. Remove from caul fat, slice and serve with roasted potatoes or polenta.

CORATELLA AI CARCIOFI

Stewed Innards with Artichokes

Yield: 4 servings

Ingredients

3 pounds	lamb innards (heart, kidney, lungs, liver)
6 small	artichokes, fresh
2 ounces	extra virgin olive oil
	salt and black pepper to taste
1 large	lemon juice only

Preparation

Cut the liver into slices and cut the other organs into pieces. Blanch the artichokes for 10 minutes, remove the leaves and beard and slice the bottom. Toss with a few drops of lemon juice, to prevent discoloring and set aside. In medium size skillet, heat the oil and add all innards except the kidney and liver. When innards are well browned and tender (about 5 minutes), add the kidney, liver and sliced artichoke bottoms and cook 2 minutes more. Add salt, pepper, and the juice of a squeezed lemon and serve immediately.

CORATELLA AI CARCIOFI

This is a combination of all the innards, made famous after the Wars. As Italy was trying to rebuild, the imagination of the Italian mamme created specialties such as this, which stands the test of time among the immigrants of Federal Hill.

CONIGLIO IN UMIDO

Stewed Rabbit

Yield: 4 servings

Ingredients

1-4 pound	rabbit, fresh, cut in pieces
6 leaves	fresh sage
1 tablespoon	fresh rosemary
1 clove	garlic, minced
3 ounce	extra virgin olive oil
	salt and black pepper
	to taste
6	juniper berries
1/2 cup	red wine vinegar

Preparation

Wash and dry rabbit. In a bowl, blend a few fresh sage leaves, rosemary, garlic, and juniper berries slightly smashed. Salt and pepper to taste. Rub the pieces of rabbit in the herbs and place in a terra cotta pot or deep baking dish. Mix together vinegar and 6 tablespoons olive oil and pour over the rabbit. Allow to marinate for 24 hours in refrigerator turning the meat occasionally so that it absorbs the flavors. Preheat oven at 400° F. Cook covered for about 45 minutes. Uncover the pot, raise the heat to 450° F., and cook for another 45 minutes or until the rabbit is tender and the liquid almost completely absorbed. Serve with roasted Swiss chard or stewed escarole.

CONIGLIO IN UMIDO

The rabbits available on the market are domestic ones. In buying rabbits, give preference to those with fur still attached to the body since air cannot cause spoilage, and the meat will maintain good color and texture. The liver is a good source for pasta ragús.

VITELLA AL GORGONZOLA

Veal with Gorgonzola Sauce

Yield: 4 servings

Ingredients

2 pounds	veal loin, thin slices
1/2 cup	dry white wine
12 pieces	asparagus tips, steamed
2 ounces	demiglace, fresh or canned
	salt and black pepper to taste
3 ounces	Gorgonzola cheese
2 1/2 ounces	unsalted butter
1 cup	whipping cream

Preparation

To prepare the sauce, place Gorgonzola in saucepan over low heat, add 1 tablespoon of butter and stir until melted. Add 1 cup whipping cream, stirring over low heat until creamy. Remove from heat and set aside.

Veal preparation:

Sauté the veal on both sides in remaining butter approximately 5 minutes. Remove from pan and set aside. Add white wine and demiglace and stir over low flame. Add veal and Gorgonzola sauce. Stir. Season with salt and pepper to taste. Cook over low heat approximately 2 minutes. Remove and serve hot, garnished with steamed asparagus spears on the side.

VITELLA AL GORGONZOLA

I simply love the taste of different cheeses in sauces. Gorgonzola cheese is made from whole cow's milk. The cheese is very soft, sometimes creamy, and white or yellowish in color. The crust is reddish, rough, uniform and wrapped in aluminum foil. It is a specialty of Lombardia in Northern Italy, sometimes called Erborinato from the Latin "erbor", parsley, in the Milanese dialect.

TROTELLA RIPIENA

Stuffed Trout

Yield: 4 servings

Ingredients

4	trout, 20-24 ounces each
2 small	shallots, chopped
3 ounces	fresh white mushrooms, sliced
3 tablespoons	fresh Italian parsley, minced
salt to taste	
6 whole	peppercorns, left whole
1 small	carrot, diced
1 small	onion, diced
1 stalk	celery, diced
1 cup	white wine
2 1/2 ounces	unsalted butter, softened

TROTELLA RIPIENA

Trout is a fresh water fish of many varieties. The brown trout lives in cold, clear mountain rivers or lakes. Its body is agile and sturdy and the color varies according to the environment. Rainbow trout has a body more slender, and a head slightly smaller. It can be found in mountain streams as well as lowland lakes.

Preparation

In a bowl combine shallots, mushrooms and parsley. Salt to taste, add peppercorns and half of the butter cut into pea-sized pieces. Prepare a smooth mixture, then stuff the fish with it. Put the onion, carrot and celery into a fish poacher; lay the trout on top and cover with white wine. Cook on top of stove over low heat. When trout is cooked, about 15 minutes, remove from poacher and set aside. Allow to cool slightly. Remove skin, place in a serving platter and keep warm. Strain the cooking liquid, reduce over low heat, then add the unsalted butter whisking vigorously to prevent separation. When the sauce is very hot, adjust seasonings, pour over trout and serve immediately.

Note: You may create your own fish poacher by using a perforated flat pan that fits into a roasting pan. Cover with aluminum foil.

LUMACHETTE CINQUETERRE

Snails Ligurian Style

Yield: 4 servings

Ingredients

5 whole	salted anchovies, minced
1 sprig	rosemary
2 cloves	garlic
2 ounces	extra virgin olive oil
48 whole	snails
4 cups	dry white wine
	salt and black pepper to taste
2 ounces	fresh basil, minced
4 large	crostini (croutons)

Preparation

In a large skillet sauté the anchovies with rosemary and garlic in olive oil for 5 minutes. Add the snails. Stir and moisten with white wine, 1 cup at a time. When the wine evaporates, add salt and pepper and continue to cook for 30 minutes over low heat, moistening with more wine when necessary.

Before serving, add the fresh basil and serve snails on crostini topped with its own sauce.

Variation: Finely sliced mushrooms may be added after moistening with the wine. On Federal Hill, snails are sometimes served with marinara. In this version add 1 cup of fresh strained tomato before adding the snails.

LUMACHETTE CINQUETERRE

Snails are considered to be a land mollusk. They are protected by a spiral shell within which they can remain for many months. The best variety are called Vignerole, which live on grape vines, and are themselves best from October through March. Vignerole are not easily digestible, due to the meat itself and the strong ingredients used to prepare them. Although these can be found in the States, prepare this recipe with an expert on handling snails, as the process of cleaning (spurgatura) can be tiring and time consuming.

AVVOLTI DI PESCE SPADA

Swordfish Rolls

Yield: 4 servings

Ingredients

1 large	onion, chopped
1 clove	garlic, chopped
	extra virgin olive oil
2 tablespoons	fresh Italian parsley, chopped
2 tablespoons	fresh basil, chopped
1 tablespoon	capers
3 ounces	sharp Provolone cheese, diced
2 large	eggs, whole
	salt and black pepper to taste
3 ounces	fine breadcrumbs
2 pounds	Swordfish, cut into very thin slices and trimmed

AVVOLTI DI PESCE SPADA

This fish needs no introduction as the best Swordfish in the United States is probably from New England. Immigrant Italians, especially Sicilians, have a multitude of techniques and recipes, since the area in Sicily around Messina is the 'Swordfish capital' in Europe. Here we have a preparation with the unusual addition of cheese (Provolone), typical of the Italo-American culinary influence.

Preparation

Note: Trimmings should not be less than 8 ounces in weight.

Chop and brown the onion, garlic and swordfish trimmings in 1 tablespoon oil. Add the parsley, fresh basil, breadcrumbs and capers. Cook for 2 minutes, remove from heat, cool, and pass through a food mill. Combine mixture with the cheese and eggs. Salt and pepper to taste. Place swordfish between 2 pieces of wax paper. Flatten the fillets slightly, with a mallet and place a spoonful of filling in the middle. Roll up the fillets and close with toothpicks. Cook the Swordfish rolls for 8 minutes by either grilling or sautéeing in olive oil. Serve on leaves of Belgian endive with Salmoriglio sauce (a mixture of lemon juice, fresh oregano and olive oil).

CALAMARI FARCITI

Stuffed Squid

Yield: 4 servings

Ingredients

2 pounds	fresh squid, left whole
2 cloves	garlic, minced
2 tablespoons	extra virgin olive oil
6 large	pitted black olives
2 tablespoons	fresh Italian parsley, chopped
	pinch of peperoncino (hot pepper)
1 tablespoon	breadcrumbs, finely ground
2 tablespoons	Parmigiano Reggiano, grated
	pinch of oregano
1 pound	tomatoes, peeled, seeded and, chopped
1 cup	white wine, dry
1 tablespoon	capers, drained
	salt and black pepper to taste

CALAMARI FARCITI

Farcire derives from the Latin farcio which means "to fill or stuff".

Preparation

Clean the calamari by removing the eyes, beak, fin and clean inside of the sac. Wash until they become white. Remove the tentacles, chop and set aside. Sauté one garlic clove, olives, capers, parsley and peperoncino in olive oil. When golden brown, add the chopped calamari tentacles and sauté for 5 minutes over medium heat. Remove from fire and cool; add the breadcrumbs and cheese, mixing until smooth. Lightly stuff the calamari bodies with this mixture, avoid overstuffing or they will explode while cooking. Sew the opening of the sac with a needle and a colorless thread or close it with a toothpick. Sauté the remaining garlic clove in oil, add the tomatoes, a pinch of oregano, salt and pepper. Cook for 10 minutes. Place the calamari in the sauce, cover and cook gently over low heat for another 30 minutes, adding the wine if too dry.

Serve on platter over toasted country bread.

CALAMARI IN ZIMINO

Squid & Swiss Chard

Yield: 4 servings

Ingredients

2 pounds	Swiss chard (white)
7 ounces	tomatoes, peeled and seeded
1 medium	onion, finely chopped
1 stalk	celery, finely chopped
2 ounces	extra virgin olive oil
	salt and black pepper to taste
1 pound	fresh squid (calamari)
1 tablespoon	fresh Italian parsley, chopped

Preparation

To prepare the Chard, remove the outer larger leaves and wash, cut into pieces, and set aside. Sauté onion and celery in 2 ounces of oil in a saucepan until tender but not brown. Add Swiss chard, tomatoes, salt and pepper. Stir. Cover and cook over medium heat for 30 to 40 minutes. Add the squid and continue to cook for 10 minutes more over medium heat. Sprinkle generously with chopped parsley and serve directly from saucepan.

Note: This recipe can also be used with cuttlefish, known to Italian immigrants as Seppia.

CALAMARI IN ZIMINO

Zimino is a sauce of minced greens, garlic and olive oil. It may be used for vegetables or seafood. There is nothing Swiss about the chard. This green grows well in the spring, with big leaves and thin veins, and the white variety can be substituted for spinach. The red variety is used primarily for pasta and side dishes, served alone, since it may stain other foods.

TORTINO DI CICCIOLI

Ciccioli Pie

Yield: 4 servings

Ingredients

8 ounces	all-purpose flour
7 ounces	unsalted butter, room temperature
1 ounce	compressed yeast
3 large	eggs, whole
1/2 pound	ciccioli
	salt to taste

Preparation

Make a cone of flour on the pastry board with a cavity on the top.

Dissolve the yeast in a few tablespoons of lukewarm water and pour into the cavity. Add a pinch of salt, butter, eggs and half of the ciccioli, coarsely chopped. Knead the ingredients together until the dough is no longer sticky, adding more flour if necessary. Butter an 8" cake pan with high edges, stretch the dough until it covers the bottom and the sides, then sprinkle with the remaining ciccioli. Cover and set in a warm place until risen double in size, about 1 hour in a draft-free area. Cook in a preheated 400° F. oven for 30 minutes.

Note: A favorite merenda (snack) for children after school.

TORTINO DI CICCIOLI

Ciccioli are the solid particles which remain after melting bacon. (When melting, the bacon should always be chopped). Another post-war culinary expression of the Italians, yet among the Italians on Federal Hill, it was customary to purchase the dough from their favorite baker then assemble the recipe at home.

PEPERONI RIPIENI DI FUNGHI

Peppers Stuffed with Mushrooms

Yield: 4 servings

Ingredients

6 whole	yellow peppers
4 tablespoons	porcini mushrooms, dried
1 1/2 cups	stale bread, crusts removed
1 large	egg, whole
	salt and pepper to taste
5 tablespoons	Grana Padano cheese, grated
1/2 cup	extra virgin olive oil

PEPERONI RIPIENI DI FUNGHI

Grana is similar to Parmigiano, but it is produced year-round in the area north of the Po river from the skim milk of hay-fed cows. The crust is hard, occasionally dark, and oily. It is used in the same way as Parmigiano, and is a much less expensive substitute.

Preparation

Preheat the oven to 350° F. Roast the peppers. Place them in a brown paper bag. Seal and set aside for 15 minutes. Remove the skins and rinse them in water. Remove the stems, seeds and filaments, keeping the peppers whole, and place on a kitchen towel to dry. Soak the mushrooms in warm water then carefully wash them. Soak the bread in water, then squeeze out excess moisture. Put the mushrooms and bread in a blender, add the egg, a pinch each of salt and pepper, and the grated Grana.

Blend to a thick paste. Stuff the peppers with the paste and place in a terra cotta pot or deep baking dish, standing upright on their bases. Baste with oil and bake the peppers in a 350° F. oven for at least 30 minutes. Serve arranged on a platter.

Note: The sealed brown paper bag allows the pepper to cook fully and peel easily.

PETTO DI TACCHINO

Neapolitan Turkey Breast

Yield: 6 servings

Ingredients

3 pounds	turkey breast, fresh
2 tablespoons	unsalted butter
7 ounces	mozzarella cheese, fresh
4	tomatoes, peeled, seeded and julienned
	salt and black pepper to taste
2 tablespoons	fresh Italian parsley, chopped

Preparation

Preheat the oven to 400° F. Poach the turkey breast in water, let it cool and cut into thin slices. Place the turkey slices in a buttered terra cotta pot or baking dish. Cut the mozzarella in slices and arrange atop the turkey. Arrange tomatoes atop the cheese, sprinkle with salt and pepper and dot with bits of unsalted butter. Cook in a 400° F. for about 20 minutes or until the cheese melts. Remove from oven, sprinkle with parsley and serve.

PETTO DI TACCHINO

Young turkey is preferred and the preparation is much similar to cooking veal. Baste frequently to prevent birds from overcooking. Turkeys are always preferred at Christmas dinners.

VINO COTTO

Cooked Wine

Yield: 3 gallons

Ingredients

30 pounds   sweet black grapes

Method

Crush grapes to extract liquid. Strain and measure the liquid extracted. Bring liquid to a rapid boil and quickly remove foam as it forms with a stainless steel spoon.

When liquid is clear, lower heat to boil slowly. Reduce liquid to 1/3 original amount.

One hour before removing liquid from heat, fold in 2 apples (cut in quarters, seeds removed and cored) and 1 persimmon (cut in quarters).

Check consistency by spooning small portion in a plate. Liquid should be the thickness of maple syrup at this point.

Note: Ordinary table wine cannot be used.

VINO COTTO

Vino cotto is made during the wine season. An old tradition suggests that the wine is uncorked at the 21st birthday of the eldest son. The wine develops a thick-syrup consistency, and is extremely high in alcohol.

FREGOLATA VENEZIANA

Almond and Polenta Cake

Yield: 6 servings

Ingredients

1/2 cup	granulated sugar
7 tablespoons	unsalted butter, melted and cooled
2 large	egg yolks
2 teaspoons	lemon juice
1 teaspoon	vanilla extract
	grated zest of 1 lemon
1 teaspoon	almond extract
7/8 cup	fine yellow or white cornmeal
3/4 cup	all-purpose flour, scant
1 pinch	salt
	unsalted butter for greasing pan
1/4 cup	skinned, toasted almonds (or blanched almonds)
1/4 cup	skinned, toasted hazelnuts coarsely chopped
2 tablespoons	brown sugar, preferably unrefined

Preparation

In a blender or food processor fitted with a steel blade grind 1 cup of almonds with 2 to 3 tablespoons of granulated sugar to a coarse powder.

Add the remaining granulated sugar and process to a very fine powder. Transfer the almond powder to the bowl of a mixer or a large mixing bowl and beat in the unsalted butter until blended.

Add the egg yolks, lemon juice, lemon zest, and vanilla and almond extracts; mix until well blended. Add cornmeal, flour, and salt to the almond mixture and stir just until the dough comes together.

FREGOLATA VENEZIANA

The word may derive from "fregare", to rub together.

It is very important not to overwork the dough. Preheat the oven to 350° F. Butter a 9" or 10" tart or quiche pan, preferably with a removable bottom. Spread the dough in the pan, using your fingers to distribute to edges. Sprinkle with the chopped nuts and brown sugar. Bake for 5 minutes. Reduce the heat to 300° F. and bake for 45 to 50 minutes longer, until the surface is a pale golden brown.

Cool completely on a rack and cut into wedges to serve.

This Patron Saint Celebration is still carried on today, in other sections of Rhode Island. Not only were Patron Saint Processions and Celebrations held on Federal Hill but also in Knightsville, Cranston, Johnston and Thornton and wherever large groups of Italians settled. It was an occasion that brought those from a particular section of Italy together, preparing for the annual celebration of their hometown Patron Saint. It was a little bit of Italy brought to Rhode Island.

SUSEMIELLE

Cookies from Caserta

Yield: 24 cookies

Ingredients

15 ounces	molasses
1 cup	vegetable oil
2 large	eggs, beaten
1 cup	sugar, granulated
1/2 teaspoon	baking soda
6-7 cups	all-purpose flour
1 teaspoon	salt
1 tablespoon	black pepper
5 whole	orange rind, grated (about 1/2 cup)
1 cup	hazelnuts, whole

Preparation

In a bowl mix molasses, oil, eggs, sugar, baking soda, salt, pepper and orange rind. Blend well. Add flour to form a dough which can be rolled. Oil fingers; take pieces of dough and roll like a pencil. Shape roll into a 4 to 5" 'S' shape. Place hazelnuts on top and bottom of shaped dough.

Bake on a greased cookie sheet at 375° F. for 15 minutes, or until brown.

They said:
We had no running water, and no hot water.
I used to get up in the morning, and start the stove
with the charcoal leftover from the day before.

BISCOTTINI AI PIGNOLI

Pine Nut Cookies

Yield: 48 cookies

Ingredients

2 pounds	almond paste
1 1/2 cups	confectioners sugar
8 egg whites	room temperature
1 pound pignoli	(pine nuts)
1 1/2 cups	sugar, granulated
2 tablespoons	honey
1/4 teaspoon	vanilla extract

Preparation

Cream together the almond paste, sugars and honey into a smooth batter.

Beat the egg whites until stiff, gradually mixing into the batter along with the vanilla.

Spread the pignoli in a dish. Drop batter by teaspoonful into the nuts, then place onto a lightly greased cookie sheet at 1" intervals.

Bake in preheated 350° F. oven for 12 -15 minutes or until golden. Remove carefully from baking sheet with spatula while still warm.

By 1920 Italians recorded the largest number of foreign-born of any ethnic group in the State of Rhode Island. As they poured into the port of Providence on the ships of the Fabre Line, they soon replaced the Irish on Federal Hill and spread to Eagle Park and Charles Street, the North End of the city.

PANELLE

A Sicilian Traditional Snack

Yield: 24 panelle

Ingredients

4 cups	chickpea flour
6 cups	water
1 teaspoon	salt
	vegetable oil for frying

Preparation

Put chickpea flour in a saucepan and add water very slowly, stirring carefully to avoid lumps. Add salt, cook over medium heat, stirring constantly for about 15 minutes until mixture is very thick.

PANELLE

Usually served in celebration of the feast of Santa Lucia.

Pour mixture onto a lightly oiled marble or wooden surface and spread it out quickly with an oiled spatula into a thin sheet, 1/4" thick. When cool cut into 2" X 3" rectangles.

Fry the panelle in hot oil, a few at a time, turn once until both sides are golden brown. Drain on paper towel. Serve hot.

Notable was the rapid growth between 1900 and 1930 of Italian operated businesses on Providence's Federal Hill. During that time more than 35 percent of Italian shopkeepers owned their own businesses-general stores, clothing stores, and bakeries-while others served the Italian community as independent craftsmen, such as barbers, tailors, cobblers, carpenters and tinsmiths. These entrepreneurs gave the Italian Americans of Federal Hill a relatively high rate of upward economic mobility.

FRITTI AL MOSCATO

Fried Dough with Moscato Wine

Yield: Many, varies with shape

Ingredients

1 cup	vegetable oil
1 cup	moscato wine
4 cups	all-purpose flour
1 teaspoon	cinnamon
	vegetable oil for frying
6 tablespoons	honey

Preparation

In a medium saucepan, mix oil and wine, bring to a boil and cool. In a large bowl mix flour and cinnamon. Make a well and add cooled liquid slowly, working with your fingers to form a soft, pliable dough.

Break off pieces of dough and roll into long thin rope. Cut into 1" pieces, roll gently on a grooved board or make ridges with the tines of a fork.

Drop the dough pieces in hot oil a few at a time, and fry until golden. Drain on brown paper.

When cool, pour honey over top and serve.

FRITTI AL MOSCATO

Served at Christmas time, often topped with colored 'jimmies', or sprinkles.

SORBETTO AL MELONE

Melon Sherbet

Yield: 6 servings

Ingredients

1 tablespoon	honey
3 tablespoons	fresh lemon juice
1 cup	sugar, granulated
1 cup	water
3 medium ripe	cantaloupes
3 tablespoons	melon liqueur

Preparation

Bring honey, lemon juice, sugar, and water to a boil over medium heat. Cook for 5 minutes. Allow to cool.

Seed the cantaloupes. With a melon scoop make 18 cantaloupe balls. Soak the melon balls in brandy. Set aside for garnish.

Cut the rest of the cantaloupe flesh into 1" pieces and puree in a food processor until there are 3 cups of puree.

SORBETTO AL MELONE

Sicilians gave us the pleasures of gelati and sorbetti. Some of them opened ice cream shops in Providence much before the end of the Great Depression. The word sorbetto is from the Arabian "sharbia", or drink. Another message left behind by the presence of the Arabs in what the Romans called "Trinacria" or three points, geographically associated with the shape of Sicily.

Combine the cooled honey-sugar syrup and the cantaloupe puree. Mix well and freeze in an ice cream machine according to manufacturer's instructions. Transfer to a plastic container and store in the freezer until needed, no more than three days.

Allow the frozen sorbet to thaw slightly before serving to enhance the flavor. Serve with brandied cantaloupe balls and fresh mint leaves as garnish.

Note: Honeydew melon may be substituted, but lime juice must be substituted for lemon juice.

Pushcart Row, Arthur Avenue, later Balbo Avenue, today De Pasquale Avenue. Pushcarts were lined on both sides of the street where, the greatest variety of fresh fruit and vegetables could be purchased. They were opened for business from 8:30 a.m. to 9:00 p.m. Many new arrival Sicilians became the vendors. In this photo, there are several members of the Sasso Family. In the upper center of photo is where Spruce Street crossed Balbo Avenue. Circa 1920.

SFINGI DI SAN GIUSEPPE

St. Joseph's Puffs

Yield: 24 puffs

Ingredients

1/2 cup	unsalted butter
1 cup	water, boiling
1/8 teaspoon	salt
4 large	eggs, whole
1 cup	flour, all-purpose

Preparation

Put butter and water in a saucepan. Bring to boil. Mix flour and salt, adding all at once. Mix well, stirring constantly until mixture is smooth and shiny, and leaves the sides of the pan.

Remove from heat. Add whole eggs, one at a time, beating vigorously after each egg.

Drop a teaspoon of batter on greased baking sheet, spaced 2" apart.

Bake at 400° F. for 35 minutes or until nicely browned. Remove puffs and cool.

Ricotta filling:

1 pound	ricotta cheese, fresh
1/4 teaspoon	almond extract
1/2 cup	sugar, granulated
2 ounces	unsweetened chocolate, grated

Combine ricotta and sugar; mix well. Stir in grated chocolate and almond extract. When cool, cut side of each puff. Fill with ricotta filling.

CUCCUREDDI

Fig Rings

Ingredients

2 orange peels	without pith
2 cups	sugar, granulated
3 cups	water

Boil water, sugar and orange peels about 15 minutes. Set aside.

Filling:

3 pounds	dried figs
3/4 cup	sherry wine
1 teaspoon	cinnamon
1 pound	shelled almonds, roasted
1 teaspoon	nutmeg
1 teaspoon	black pepper

Cut figs into quarters; remove stems. Add boiled orange peelings and water. Soak overnight.

Dough:

12 cups	all-purpose flour
1 1/2 cups	margarine
	water as needed
1 teaspoon	salt
2 cups	sugar, granulated

Preparation

Cut margarine in cubes and blend with flour, sugar and salt. Add water to create a workable pie dough. Knead dough until smooth. Roll into a ball, cover, and let rest about 1 hour. Roll dough into a square 1/8" thickness an 12" long. Cut strips 2 3/4" wide and 12" long. Spread fig mixture in the center of each strip (about the size of a thumb). Bring the long edges of the dough together to seal. Cut filled dough in half. Form each piece into a ring and tuck the ends under. With a pair of scissors snip the top of the ring in several places, brush with beaten egg yolk. Continue with remaining strips. Place on a greased cookie sheet about 1" apart. Bake in a preheated oven at 325° F. for 20 minutes, or until dough is golden brown.

BISCOTTI AL CIOCCOLATO CON MANDORLE

Chocolate & Almond Biscotti

Yield: 24 biscotti

Ingredients

2 cups (8 oz.)	walnut halves
3 ounces	unsweetened chocolate
5 tablespoons	unsalted butter plus
1 teaspoon	unsalted butter
2 cups	all purpose flour
2 teaspoons	baking powder
3 large	eggs
1 cup	sugar, granulated
1 teaspoon	orange zest, grated

Preparation

Preheat oven to 350° F.

Place walnuts on a cookie sheet and toast until golden brown, about 10 minutes. Let cool and then chop coarsely.

In a double boiler over simmering water, melt the chocolate and butter together. Remove from heat and stir until smooth. Let cool for 10 minutes. Sift together flour and baking powder. In a large bowl, beat eggs lightly. Gradually beat in sugar; add orange zest. Stir in the cooled chocolate until blended. Stir in flour and baking powder until incorporated. Fold in chopped walnuts. Divide dough in half, wrap in plastic wrap and refrigerate at least 1 hour or overnight. Butter a large cookie sheet and preheat oven to 350° F. Shape each half of the dough into a 14" x 2 1/2" log. Place about 4 inches apart on the prepared pan. Smooth the tops and sides with a rubber spatula. Bake for 40-45 minutes, or until the logs are firm when pressed in the center. Remove the baking sheet from the oven. Do not turn off the oven. Slide the logs onto a cutting board. With a large knife, cut each log diagonally into 1/2" slices. Stand the slices upright on edge on the prepared cookie sheet. Return to the oven and bake for 15 minutes longer or until crisp. Transfer to wire racks to cool completely.

GELATO DI MIRTILLI

Blueberry Gelato

Yield: 8 servings (1 quart)

Ingredients

2/3 cup	sugar
4	egg yolks
1 cup	milk, room temperature
1 pinch	salt
1	lemon peel strip (2")
2 cups	fresh blueberries, pureed or frozen puree
1 cup	heavy cream

Preparation

Beat sugar and egg yolks together until pale yellow and very thick. Slowly add milk, beating gently to avoid a build-up of foam. Add lemon peel and stir in salt. Transfer mixture to the top of a double boiler with 1" of boiling water in the bottom half.

Maintain water at a low boil and stir continuously for 8 minutes. Custard will thicken to coat the spoon, and surface foam will disappear. Immediately remove top of double boiler and set it in a large bowl of cold water. Stir 2 minutes to cool custard. Transfer to a bowl, cover, and chill thoroughly. Chill pureed blueberries and heavy cream. When ready to proceed, whip cream into soft peaks. Remove lemon peel from custard and fold in blueberries and whipped cream.

Transfer mixture to ice cream machine and freeze according to manufacturer's directions.

GELATO DI MIRTILLI

According to my historical research, gelato has very ancient origins. It is believed that the Arabs introduced gelato to the Western World through Sicily. The Greeks and the Turks were also known for preparing lemon-based mixtures that resembled sorbetto (sherbets).

CROSTATA DI FRUTTA DI STAGIONE

Fresh Fruit Tart

Yield: 6 servings

Ingredients

Shortcake:

7 ounces	all-purpose flour
2 1/2 ounces	granulated sugar
1 pinch	salt
3 1/2 ounces	unsalted butter
2	egg yolks
1/4 teaspoon	lemon rind, grated

Pastry cream:

3	egg yolks
1/3 cup	granulated sugar
2 ounces	all-purpose flour
1 teaspoon	vanilla flavoring
1 1/2 cups	milk, whole

Preparation

Sift together flour, sugar, and salt on a wooden pastry board. Make a well in the center and add butter, egg yolks, and lemon rind. Mix and knead with fingertips taking care not to overwork the dough. When smooth, shape into a ball and chill for about 30 minutes. Roll out lightly in a circle; cut edges of dough about 1 inch larger than 8" to 9" diameter fluted flan tin. Butter and flour the pan and fit the pastry into it, again trim the edges, prick with fork and flute edges. Place in preheated oven at moderate heat for 15 to 20 minutes.

For crema pasticcera:

Beat together yolks and sugar until thick, and light lemon in color. Beat in flour and vanilla. Over medium heat, bring milk just to boil. Let cool for a moment, then add to egg mixture, whisking rapidly. Cook over low heat until the pastry cream thickens enough to coat the back of a wooden spoon. Cool. When cream pasticcera is cool, spread evenly on the bottom of the pie. Fill with whatever fresh fruits are available; melt apricot jam in a small amount of hot water and glaze tart to finish.

Arthur Avenue, Balbo Avenue today De Pasquale Avenue. A typical street scene where everyone met and purchased daily fruit and vegetables. From left to right today exists, the Cappelli Building, Trainor Street and the Mastrobonno's Jewelry Company. Children at an early age would go shopping with their parents. It became a familiar scene where an entire family sometimes went shopping for the week's supply of fruit and vegetables.

CROSTATA DI FICHI E LAMPONI

Crostata of Figs & Raspberries

Yield: 10 servings

Ingredients
Sweet dough:

1 cup	all-purpose flour
1/4 cup	sugar
1 pinch	salt
1/4 teaspoon	baking powder ,
1/4 cup	unsalted butter
1 large	egg

Almond cream filling:

1/4 pound	almond paste
1/4 cup	sugar, granulated
1	egg yolk
4 tablespoons	unsalted butter, room temperature
1 large	egg
3 tablespoons	flour, all-purpose
12	ripe figs peeled and quartered
1/2 pint	raspberries, fresh
	confectioners sugar for dusting

Preparation

For the dough: Preheat oven to 350° F. Combine dry ingredients in bowl of food processor and pulse several times to mix. Cut unsalted butter into 8 pieces and distribute evenly over dry ingredients in work bowl. Pulse until very finely powdered. Add egg and continue to pulse until dough forms a ball that revolves on blade. Remove dough, press into a disk, wrap and chill.

For the almond filling: Combine almond paste, sugar and yolk and beat by machine until smooth. Beat in butter, scrape bowl and beaters and beat in egg. Continue beating until light. Stir in flour. Roll dough on a floured surface and line a 10" tart pan. Spread filling evenly in pan. Bake 40 minutes, until crust and filling are baked through. Cool on a rack. To finish the crostata, arrange the fig quarters, cut side up, in concentric rows on the baked almond filling. Lace the raspberries between the figs and in the center of the tart. Just before serving, dust with the confectioners sugar and serve.

Note: Crostata is an open-faced tart with lattice top. The name derives from the Latin word crusta (crust). In Milano, crostata is filled with pears and rum, and glazed with apricot jam; in Rome with ricotta and lemon peel, and laced with Marsala wine; in Sicily with the obvious additions of pistachio, citrus and potato starch.

MATTONELLA DI CIOCCOLATO

Chocolate Terrine

Yield: 10 servings

Ingredients

8 ounces	Belgian semi-sweet chocolate
1/3 cup	water
8 ounces	Mascarpone cheese*
1/4 cup	sugar, granulated
2 teaspoons	vanilla extract
12 ounce	whipping cream
1 tablespoon	milk
2 tablespoons	almond liqueur

Preparation

Lightly grease 8" x 4" loaf pan, lining bottom and sides with waxed paper. Melt chocolate with water in saucepan over low heat, stirring constantly. Cool slightly. Beat mascarpone and sugar until smooth. Beat in vanilla and chocolate mixture. Fold in the cream previously whipped. Stir in milk and almond liqueur. Spread into lined pan. Chill until firm, about 4 hours.

Unmold and remove waxed paper.

Note:* Mascarpone is not really a cheese but rather a very rich substance made from cream that has been soured with fermenting bacteria. It is a regional specialty of Lombardia and is produced almost exclusively during the winter. It is sold by weight and usually mixed with liqueurs, sugar, chocolate. Is also used as a filling for sweets and cakes.

TRINACRIA OPLONTIS

Cassata Cake Trinacria

Yield: 4 servings

Ingredients

3 1/2 cups	fresh ricotta
3/4 cup	honey
1/4 cup	Galliano liqueur
3 large	eggs, yolks only
1/4 cup	Alkermes (red liqueur)

Ingredients for almond paste:

4 1/2 ounces	almonds
4 1/2 ounces	sugar, granulated
1 ounce	all-purpose flour
1	egg white, unbeaten
	candied fruits; dates, prunes, tangerines

TRINACRIA OPLONTIS

The name symbolizes the region of Sicily. From the Latin "Trinacria", three points, because of its shape.

Preparation

Almond paste: Boil almonds for 8 minutes and remove skins. Grind all ingredients together in food processor to make paste.

Beat the drained ricotta with honey and Galliano (do not use sugar). Add beaten egg yolks. Prepare a spring-form mold by lining the bottom with a 8" layer of almond paste which has been tinted with Alkermes. On top place the ricotta cream and put into refrigerator. When ready, about three hours, remove from mold and decorate with candied fruit, such as dates, tangerine slices, and prunes, coated in honey.

Note: candied fruit may be substituted with green and yellow citron, available in gourmet shops.

BABA' AL RUM

Rum Babas

Yield: 12 Babas

Ingredients

Dough:

1 ounce	compressed yeast
1/2 cup	milk, whole
1/2 cup	all-purpose flour
salt	
3 large	eggs, whole
1/2 cup	unsalted butter
4 tablespoons	raisins, dark

Syrup:

3 tablespoons	sugar, granulated
1/2 cup	water
4 tablespoons	rum liqueur

Preparation

Dissolve the yeast in 1/2 cup of warm milk and make a dough with 4 tablespoons flour. Place dough in a bowl, cover, and let stand in a warm place for 30 minutes or until doubled in size. Make a fountain on a pastry board with the remaining flour, pinch of salt, eggs, sugar, unsalted butter and fermented dough. Soak the raisins in lukewarm water, squeeze and work into the dough. Put the dough in a large buttered, sugar-dusted ring mold and let rise again in a warm place until doubled in size (approximately 1 hour). Bake for 45 minutes in a 375° F. oven.

Prepare a syrup by dissolving the sugar in the water over a low flame then adding the rum. Unmold the baba while still warm. Soak with the rum syrup and serve.

Note: Small babas are made the same way by dividing the dough and cooking them in individual molds.

GENOISE CON AMARETTO

Amaretto Flavored Genoise

Yield: 4 servings

Ingredients

2/3 cup	sugar, granulated
7 large	eggs
3/4 cup	all-purpose flour
3 tablespoons	cornstarch
2 teaspoons	grated lemon rind
	amaretto/chocolate

Filling:

3 cups	whipping cream
6 ounces	semi-sweet chocolate chips
1/4 cup	Amaretto liqueur
1 - 9"	genoise, split

Preparation

For Genoise: In a bowl, mix eggs and sugar. Heat over hot water to 110° F., beating until doubled in volume. Sift flour and cornstarch together three times. Carefully fold the flour, cornstarch and lemon rind into the egg mixture. Pour into a greased and floured 9" cake pan. Bake at 425° F. until set and springy. Remove from pan and cool on cake rack.

GENOISE CON AMARETTO

Genoise is a method of blending eggs with sugar over a bain-marie. Originally it was created in Genova, and later adopted by the folks of Provence, west of Liguria.

For Filling: Heat cream to 180° F. Stir in chocolate chips and remove from the heat. Stir to melt; chill overnight. Put half of the genoise on the cake and sprinkle with half of the amaretto. Whip the cream mixture until stiff. Spread 1/4 of the mixture on the cake. Add top layer of cake and sprinkle with the remaining amaretto. Ice top and sides of cake with chocolate filling, reserving some to pipe through a pastry bag for finishing touches.

Bocce court where men of the Italian communities would gather Sunday afternoons and holidays to play their favorite pastime. This was serious business, and as times went on, teams were formed and later, the teams from Federal Hill, Natick, Thornton and throughout Rhode Island would have tournaments. This sport was very popular with Italians. It was played on the weekends and in the summertime evenings, when the days were longer, when only voices could be heard. Today, Bocce Clubs have continued but are more elaborate; indoors and illuminated. Today a public outdoor bocce court exists in the Garabaldi Park, located where the arch has been erected, at the Gateway to Federal Hill.

RECIPE LISTING